The Data Economy

"The data economy" is a term used by many, but properly understood by few. Even more so the concept of "big data." Both terms embody the notion of a digital world in which many transactions and data flows animate a virtual space. This is the unseen world in which technology has become the master, with the hand of the human less visible. In fact, however, it is human interaction in and around technology that makes data so pervasive and important – the ability of the human mind to extract, manipulate, and shape data that gives meaning to it.

This book outlines the findings and conclusions of a multidisciplinary team of data scientists, lawyers, and economists tasked with studying both the possibilities of exploiting the rich data sets made available from many human–technology interactions and the practical and legal limitations of trying to do so. It revolves around a core case study of Singapore's public transport system, using data from both the private company operating the contactless payment system (EZ-Link) and the government agency responsible for public transport infrastructure (Land Transport Authority). In analysing both the possibilities and the limitations of these data sets, the authors propose policy recommendations in terms of both the uses of large data sets and the legislation necessary to enable these uses while protecting the privacy of users.

Sree Kumar is a Director of Sreekumar Siddique & Co., a regional research and consulting firm based in Singapore. At the Lee Kuan Yew Centre for Innovative Cities, he is an Adjunct Senior Fellow. Mr Kumar holds degrees in law, economics, English, management, and engineering from universities in the United Kingdom and Singapore. He has been called to the Bar of England and Wales and has an interest in international tax and investment law. He is a Fellow of the Royal Statistical Society.

Warren B. Chik is an Associate Professor in the School of Law at Singapore Management University. He obtained his LLB from National University of Singapore Law School and his master's degrees from Tulane University and University College London. Associate Professor Chik has been called to the Bar of England and Wales, Singapore, and New York. He currently researches and writes in the areas of information and communications technology and the law, Internet intermediaries, data protection, cybersecurity, and the intersection between intellectual property and information technology law.

See-Kiong Ng is a Professor of Practice at the National University of Singapore's School of Computing and Director of Translational Research for the university's Institute of Data Science. He holds a PhD from Carnegie-Mellon University and is a practising data scientist with diverse and cross-disciplinary research interests. From using data mining to unravel the biology of the human body to applying machine learning to understand the "biology" of complex human cities, See-Kiong aims to push the boundary of data science through trans-disciplinary upstream research and to create impact by translating research outcomes into real-life applications.

Sin Gee Teo is a research scientist at the Institute for Infocomm Research (I²R) in Singapore. He holds a PhD in Computer Science from Monash University, Australia. Before joining I²R, he worked at the Lee Kuan Yew Centre for Innovative Cities, Singapore University of Technology and Design, as a research fellow. His research interests include data privacy, applied cryptography, deep learning, data mining, and cloud computing.

Routledge Research in Public Administration and Public Policy

The Data Economy
Implications from Singapore

**Sree Kumar, Warren B. Chik,
See-Kiong Ng, and Sin Gee Teo**

LONDON AND NEW YORK

First published 2019 by Routledge

2 Park Square, Milton Park, Abingdon, Oxfordshire OX14 4RN

52 Vanderbilt Avenue, New York, NY 10017

Routledge is an imprint of the Taylor & Francis Group, an informa business

First issued in paperback 2020

British Library Cataloguing in Publication Data
A catalogue record for this book is available from the British Library

Library of Congress Cataloging in Publication Data
Names: Sree Kumar, author. | Chik, Warren B., author. |
Ng, See-Kiong, author. | Teo, Sin Gee, author.
Title: The data economy : implications from Singapore /
Sree Kumar, Warren B. Chik, See-Kiong Ng and Sin Gee Teo.
Description: Abingdon, Oxon ; New York, NY : Routledge, 2018. |
Series: Routledge research in public administration and public policy ; 20 |
Includes bibliographical references and index.
Identifiers: LCCN 2018035412 | ISBN 9781138359574 (hardback) |
ISBN 9780429433658 (e-book)
Subjects: LCSH: Data mining–Economic aspects. |
Big data–Economic aspects. | Data mining–Economic aspects–Singapore. |
Big data–Economic aspects–Singapore. |
Urban transportation–Singapore–Data processing.
Classification: LCC HB143.5 .S74 2018 | DDC 338.4/700631205957–dc23
LC record available at https://lccn.loc.gov/2018035412

ISBN: 978-1-138-35957-4 (hbk)
ISBN: 978-0-367-60671-8 (pbk)

Typeset in Times
by Out of House Publishing

Contents

Illustrations

Figures

Tables

Foreword

In 2014, the Lee Kuan Yew Centre for Innovative Cities launched the "Future of Cities," a project funded by the National Research Foundation, the Urban Renewal Authority, and the National Population and Talent Division. The project comprising seven studies tries to unpack the future challenges facing Singapore and examined the policies shaping that future in different sectors. The studies covered the future economy, future society, the data economy and its implications, future transport policies, future urban typologies, sustainable futures, and living with technology. All but one of the studies have been completed and the last will be concluded soon. The completed studies are being published as journal papers or books.

The Data Economy: Implications from Singapore shows how data have become an important feature of the economy and business transactions. It is a multidisciplinary study with elements drawn from economics and business, data science, and law. The purpose is to define the makings of a data economy. The terms "data economy" and "digital economy" have become buzzwords today. There are expectations building up of how data can enhance and grow economic opportunities. This book looks at how the economic contours are shifting as data become "a general purpose technology." It presents the data economy using data analytics on urban transportation in Singapore and the legal limitations of using these data. The role of privacy law and the regulation environment are discussed with lessons learnt from Asia.

We hope this publication will prove to be useful for those seeking to understand how to engage with the data economy and the digital economy.

Chan Heng Chee
Chairman
Lee Kuan Yew Centre for Innovative Cities
Singapore University of Technology and Design
Singapore

Acknowledgements

This book is based on research funded by the National Research Foundation (NRF) in Singapore and administered through the Ministry of National Development (MND). Data for the empirical case study was provided by EZ-Link Pte Ltd and the Land Transport Authority (LTA). The authors thank these stakeholders for their support in this research.

The findings and conclusions in this book are those of the authors and do not reflect the views of the NRF, MND, EZ-Link Pte Ltd, or LTA.

1 Introduction

This book is a product of its time. The "data economy" has now become a common term, used by many and understood by few. There is a sense of mystery that shrouds the idea of a data economy, more so the concept of "big data." Both terms embody the notion of a digital world in which many transactions and data flows animate virtual space. This is the unseen world in which technology has become the master with the hand of the human less visible. However, this is to miss the wood for the trees. The human interaction in and around technology is what makes data so pervasive and important. It is the ability of the human mind to extract, manipulate, and shape data that gives meaning to it. This transformation of data into meaningful information for decision-making is central to the idea of a "data economy," and it involves the use of large and complex sets of data (i.e. big data).

This study is unusual in that it brings together a multidisciplinary team of data scientists, lawyers, and economists to construct a possible structure of a "data economy" and its evolution. From looking at how the use of data has expanded and how different entities such as governments, businesses, and individuals continue to generate and use data through various means, the study constructs the critical elements that inform the new economy. It draws on data from the transportation network[1] in Singapore to model travel patterns, number of footfalls at the different critical nodes by time of day, and segmentation of the data by parameters such as age group, gender, and tourist status. While these empirical findings are salient to the study, equally important has been the due process of obtaining data from different sources. The acquisition of data from public (Land Transport Authority [LTA]) and private (EZ-Link) sources has had its own rhythm, since they are governed by different legislative constructs. This process has also highlighted how the integration of different data sets, their curation, and their standardisation for analytics have unique complexities. These have been challenging in both their technical and legal demands. The legal requirements for confidentiality and the maintenance of privacy have, in their own ways, been strong filters through which the data sets have been obtained, anonymised, and structured for analytics. The results of these stringent demands have nevertheless been to support a robust analytics framework through which to visualise the complex movement of people through the transportation network in Singapore.

The study, while focusing on Singapore, has also drawn lessons from other jurisdictions. The use of data analytics for decision-making in urban activities is not new, but the growing cities of Asia have been at the forefront of using data in innovative ways. Seoul, Taipei, Hong Kong, Shanghai, and Tokyo are all well versed in the use of big data for urban management – even more so since these cities have embedded and embraced cashless payment systems for a variety of public and private transactions. The pool of data that they have collected is immense and some, such as Seoul, have used it in unusual ways for transport planning. Likewise, the Hong Kong transportation system (MTR Corp.) has tried to commercialise its customer database, resulting in a contested space between private and public interests. Thus, there are interesting features of data management, processing, and controls that are being explored in Asia and its metropolitan areas. There is now a rich vein of information regarding how data is being obtained and managed in Asia's urban conurbations, and this study has tapped into this knowledge base.

One of the aims of this study has been to ensure that the latest in "big data" and data analytics is being tracked. Team members have therefore attended workshops and conferences on the latest developments in these areas in the United States and Israel. Some of the ideas from these meetings have found a voice in this study and have been integrated into the analytics framework used on the data sets.

The findings in this study reflect the different elements of how data can, and eventually will, become a part of economic structure. There are already signs of change in traditional economic activities as data become more important features of business and daily life. Online shopping, Internet banking, applications in transport such as Uber, or short-term lets through Airbnb are all acting in concert to change the ways in which traditional economic activity is structured. These are, in the parlance of the technology pundits, "disruptors." While these new technology-based businesses are disrupting the marketplace, they are also redefining the deeper concepts of what a market will look like. Traditional economic theory posits the important role of the factors of production and how they are governed by rules and regulations to ensure an orderly marketplace. Land, labour, and capital were seen to be the critical factors of production in a traditional economy before being observed to have synergies that could give rise to new skills and improved productivity. As capital became better utilised through technology and innovation, the service economy emerged to become a more prevalent feature of modern society. Technology thus has facilitated the movement of large numbers from the land and from rural factories to seek livelihoods in the cities.

It is thus in the urban setting that the rules of engagement in the new marketplace are being contested and redrawn. Increasingly, data is a resource that is being used to fashion new demand and supply contours in the economy. Big data with appropriate analytics, for example, allows businesses to segment their customers, define their product lines with more precision in quality and pricing, and focus their sales to a better-defined customer base. In turn, customers have now become more discerning in their tastes as the Internet and applications on their mobile phones allow them to compare quality, design, and prices from different suppliers without leaving the home, the office, or their trains and buses. This narrowing in the asymmetry of information has its own challenges, including that of managing expectations of consumers and addressing the risks of misinterpreting vital information. This change in the structure of information can be easily ascertained in the case of medical products and medications that a supposedly "informed" consumer purchases for self-medication without proper medical supervision. Thus, the availability of data in various forms – digital, textual, visual, audio – raises several prospects for their capture, processing, manipulation, and eventual use in decision-making. The role of data analytics has, as a result, become a critical feature in the use of big data in business, policy-making, and personal decision-making.

These emerging trends portray the arrival of data as a constituent of the economic landscape. It is now a raw input into algorithms (the analytics part of the process), which then massages and manipulates that input to create value-added information. The information itself may then have to be consolidated into different frameworks so that meaningful insights can be derived from that collage. There may be significant value embedded in those insights that have come about as a result of several factors – data inputs, data processing, information extraction, framework definition and creation, and finally a human interpretation of the patterns that have emerged (i.e. the insight into a particular solution to a problem or into an understanding of the problem itself). This can best be illustrated through an example such as footfalls in a shopping mall. If data on the movement of people in a shopping mall throughout the day can be captured through an electronic gateway or a security camera, this data can be curated, verified, and structured for data analytics in order to extract important parameters such as number of footfalls per hour, gender, age, and the like. If the framework of the subsequent analysis is to identify the peak periods and the profile of the consumers, then this information can be culled through the analytics to become a part of marketing inputs for the mall. There is an inherent value to this information, in that the mall owners can design an appropriate strategy to attract more customers. If there is an increase in the number of customers as a result of this exercise, then this change in customer numbers and the attendant change in revenues captured by the retailers in the mall are reflections of the imputed value of the data, their analytics, and the interpretation of the underlying patterns.

This simple example also raises a further possibility in economic expansion. The process of collecting, verifying, and curating data, as well as running analytics, is a specialised function that requires unique skills. The idea of a data scientist is now a reality as industry and services have realised the value of data and the need to extract important insights from it. So data scientists have become sought-after specialists. The advent of cloud computing, faster processing capabilities, and machine learning have coalesced to provide data scientists with a new armoury with which to address the requirements of the marketplace. The growth of a new sector – data analytics and management – is a consequence of the widespread availability and use of data by business and government. In a similar fashion, there is also the corresponding growth in new service sectors such as cybersecurity and data protection.

The overall effect of data becoming a resource like any other and that can be used as an input for value creation is to nurture new economic sectors while allowing the current economic space to become more efficient and, often, narrowing its contours by removing obsolete activities. This Schumpeterian world of creative destruction has become more rapid as technology has diffused into many more areas of work, leisure, and production. As a result of these changes, the nature of work itself is undergoing a structural shift. More is being achieved through less physical effort, while intellectual endeavour has become more entrenched – "intellectual" in the sense that the mind has to become flexible and attuned to several tasks requiring analytical capabilities. There is thus a reduced need for physical labour and a more pronounced requirement for knowledge-intensive workers willing to participate in a digital world. This restructuring of the workforce carries with it several social responsibilities, including a need to narrow the digital divide, facilitate seamless movement across sectors, and enhance the opportunities for skills improvement. The role of public policy becomes all the more salient in this amorphous and rapidly shifting environment.

It can thus be observed that the data economy has a wide canvas of interaction within its ambit. It affects business, government, the labour market, and the consumer in a variety of ways. The interaction between the public and private spheres of activity brings to the fore the need for protecting the public interest as much as that of the individual. There is a legislative imperative to ensure that the rules and regulations that define the market-place are well designed to prevent abuses and breaches of privacy. The nature of the data economy is such that there can be a high degree of privacy loss, abuse of the due processes of governance, and the potential for a loss in trust in the institutions that govern the market. Thus, the legal contours that define the marketplace must keep pace with changes in technology and the manner in which data is being acquired for analytics and its subsequent use. The value chain of the information creation process must be policed effect-ively to prevent unlawful use and to maintain the privacy and integrity of the data that has been collected. These are onerous demands in a technology-intensive environment in which skills and capabilities for data management are in short supply. Thus, the legal perimeters of the market have to become much better defined, transparent, and neutral to allow the marketplace to function effectively.

What is becoming more visible in the new economy is the changing share of production and usage of data by the various agents – governments, pri-vate entities, and individuals. It is likely that the share of data produced and used by private agents and individuals will increase and overtake that which is contributed by governments. This is to be expected as non-government entities experiment, commercialise, and widen their reach to capture a much larger audience. However, this expansion will depend on how technology deepens and becomes cost-effective in collecting data, analysing it, and dis-seminating the resulting information. Innovation in technology and its use will therefore be a catalyst for this process to unfold. This also implies that a widening of the current skills base will be necessary so that technology is used most effectively. The calls for specialised skills within data science and its cluster of activities will increase significantly even as machine learning and artificial intelligence (AI) become more prevalent. This pro-liferation of data use and the attendant creation of new economic activities will call for better data protection, increasing demands for privacy, and a fairer marketplace. These are activities that have a significant bearing on public space and will require a stronger hand of governments. As a result, the role of governments in legislating, regulating, and overseeing the market will increase in importance. The failure of self-regulation, as has been seen in the past, is an indicator of how intensive this intervention will need to be in order to balance public and private interests. A new concord of rules and regulations that govern the data economy may be the outcome of this need for greater policing of the new virtual world.

This book explores these possibilities and defines some of these changes in the light of the empirical evidence obtained from the Singapore transportation data. More so, it also looks at the legal contours that define these activities through lessons learnt from other jurisdictions.

Taken together, the results of this study posit the evolution of the data economy in the context of a city economy and the challenges it poses for decision-makers.

Note

1   Data has been provided by the Land Transport Authority (LTA) and its commercial subsidiary, EZ-Link, for this study.

2 An outline of the data economy

Data has now become a fixed feature of most economic activities. It is being captured through various means – digital, textual, visual, and, in some cases, audio technologies. The amount of data collected is vast compared to the amount that is actually analysed and used for decision-making. This is not surprising since the tendency to collect is often all-encompassing because of the uncertainty associated with how useful data may be in the future. As a result, there is much more data available in different forms than is actually analysed and acted upon. Nevertheless, this large pool of data has now become a form of raw "input" for sophisticated analysis from which deep insights can be gained. There are now comparisons with how oil became a feedstock for many of the world's industries.[1]

Just as oil is the base for many industrial activities, data has now become the input for many services and industries that are interconnected through digital pathways. But the comparison with oil or other such similar input runs into some obstacles when it is observed that valuing and establishing ownership of data can sometimes be more difficult than in the case of physical products. This is partly due to the nature of data that is not readily countable, the influence of network effects, and the presence of information asymmetries. However, if data is to be seen as an integral part of the new economy, then it must also exhibit, or be a part of, some of the features of an economic system. This chapter will look at several elements that constitute a structure that can be termed a "data economy."

The elements of a data economy

A traditional economy is defined as having the factors of production – land, labour, and capital – being used in a formulaic manner so as to create outputs from specific input materials. A market for these outputs (and for inputs as well) is then created for beneficial exchange through transactions that can be barter trade or, in a more sophisticated case, through a monetary exchange of some form. As the number of producers changes, such as through mergers or acquisitions, there may arise oligopolies or monopolies that arise to control the quantity and price of products. The same can be true in the provision of services that use labour and capital in some unique combination. In both instances, government intervention becomes necessary to prevent abuse of market power and to protect the public interest, which in this case will also include the many other smaller producers who are also consumers. However, governments also intervene to ensure that the public interest is protected for other reasons as well, such as safety, health, and orderly market behaviour. This rudimentary example highlights the different participants in an economy – producers, consumers, and governments – and also the ways in which the hand of government may be an important feature of managing the marketplace. But the fundamental assumption in this example is also that the raw materials for production are also available through some market mechanism that exists within or outside the immediate economic space. Data now takes the place of raw materials, as it has become a common currency within the marketplace. It is produced by almost every transaction and is not just a discarded output, but a valuable input for extracting insights that can generate subsequent value. As individuals, firms, and governments recognise the importance of data, a market for data is now emerging. This is not to suggest it is a replacement for the real goods and services sectors, but an augmentation of the current economic structure, with data becoming an important ingredient in creating and, in some cases, destroying value.

A data economy will therefore also exhibit some of the features discussed above. Data is the raw material in a data economy, and it is important to discern the subtle difference between a data economy and a digital economy. Both depend on information technology and computing capabilities. In a digital economy, this involves the conversion of a manual process into a digitised one in which computers handle what was once a largely manual activity. The move from adding machines and ledgers to a computer-based accounting system in which many of the computations are automated is the creation of a digital process. But there is still an element of manual data entry that precedes the actual computations by the machine. So, for example, there are sales data inputs, pricing, stock controls, and other variables that have to be fed into the computer for this to work. If there could be sensors that transmit the sales of items and their pricing directly from the item into the tills that also collect data on the payment mode, time, and day, and all this data is then captured automatically by a computer system that analyses the sales, revenues, costs, and the like, then we have moved from a digital world into the data world. Indeed, this is how the data economy becomes a reality. A credit card transaction, for example, captures a host of data sets that define that transaction for a particular purpose. It records the name of the buyer, his or her unique account number, the place, date, and time of the transaction, the merchant, and the product or service that has been bought. A collection of such data for that one credit card holder provides a deep insight into his or her preferences and buying behaviour. When such data is aggregated for a large number of card holders and over different time horizons, the credit card company has access to patterns of card holder behaviour, and also to the relative merits of different merchants. As the card company has access to personal data on many card holders, it can also segment its card holder base by gender, age, profession, income group, buying behaviour, and creditworthiness, among others. This rich data set is derived from the fact that the transactions have gone beyond just being a digital activity to one that generates several dimensions of card holder behaviour. This, however, is only a simple example of a basic credit card transaction. Another, less apparent, example of the difference between digitisation and datafication can be seen in the way Google has digitised texts and then datafied them by using optical character recognition to identify and recognise the letters, words, sentences, and paragraphs in the text.[2] Many other forms of data capture are now possible – analogue, digital, visual, textual, and audio – making data collection and retrieval a complex process. As the capacity for storage has increased and the amount of complex data has exploded, these large data sets become a part of "big data," which has been defined by one author[3] as "the collection of large, complex and diverse sets of data" (Figure 2.1).

Big data is now a part of business vocabulary and the advantages of using it are being touted far and wide. There is no doubt that big data, in its different forms, is useful for decision-making. Much of that data, however, has to be filtered, curated, and, in many cases, structured for analysis before it can become useful. The use of high-speed computing, cloud services, refined sensors, and fast communications is a prerequisite for this to work. It is the coalescence of these features in the digital industry that makes data collection and its use feasible in a cost-effective manner. Thus, big data can be seen as a subset of the digital industry. It provides a far deeper perspective of patterns and trends within society and allows for the observance of market transactions and behaviour. There is now a richness in data that can be extracted, analysed, and interpreted for decision-making. These possibilities depend on how well the processes for interacting with the data, conducting analytics, and the subsequent interpretation can be seamlessly integrated. Indeed, the value chain of data collection, transmission, analytics, and output generation has become almost seamless for many dedicated processes. In the parlance of economists, these activities have now become frictionless or have low or negligible transaction costs.[4] As

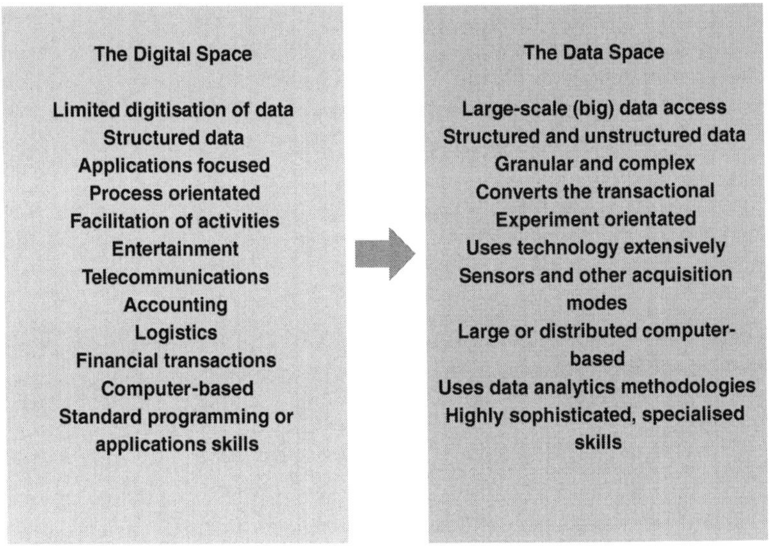

The Digital Space	The Data Space
Limited digitisation of data Structured data Applications focused Process orientated Facilitation of activities Entertainment Telecommunications Accounting Logistics Financial transactions Computer-based Standard programming or applications skills	Large-scale (big) data access Structured and unstructured data Granular and complex Converts the transactional Experiment orientated Uses technology extensively Sensors and other acquisition modes Large or distributed computer-based Uses data analytics methodologies Highly sophisticated, specialised skills

Figure 2.1 The transformation of the digital space
Source: Authors

the barriers to entry have declined significantly and transaction costs have become negligible, there has been a proliferation of different entities providing a variety of capabilities within big data. There are companies that provide data capture services, those that provide storage, those that specialise in secure transmission, and those that provide cybersecurity. Amidst these, there are those that focus on data analytics and interpretation. While there are large corporates such as Google, Amazon, and Microsoft that have a full service capability, there are many others with niche capabilities in the world of big data. The marketplace of big data service providers has, as a consequence, become fragmented, with a few large players and plethora of smaller companies providing specialised services. The effect of this change has been for large industrial and service companies to outsource several of their previously in-house-maintained capabilities. It is now common, for example, for data processing, storage, and analytics to be done by an outsourced company. This change is driven by the fact that internal transaction costs are higher than externally sourced services. The result of this structural change in firms, when seen across the industrial and service landscape, is a drastically changing economic structure led by the Internet revolution.[5]

As the shift from a hierarchical industrial structure to a flat and networked structure of industries and services takes hold, the nature of work itself changes. Repetitive tasks are being automated, while even once highly professional services such as accounting and law are being invaded by AI, which can sift through masses of big data to identify important patterns, precedents, and immediate trends. The change is essentially towards a new class of knowledge-intensive work, that which requires creative and quantitative skills. Thus, the data economy as it emerges brings together several threads of important changes – a fluctuating shift in industry structure as smaller firms become entrenched in niche sectors, as larger firms become powerful and dominant, as labour becomes more specialised and knowledge-intensive, as consumers become more active participants in data generation and its use, and as governments face the challenge of policing the new boundaries of the marketplace. Much of how these changes crystallise and support a new economic structure is also being driven by technology and the pace at which new technical advances are being adapted and incorporated into the marketplace. Thus, this shifting economic landscape provides several lenses through which to perceive the data economy.

At a broad level, there are three major sets of players – governments, private entities, and individuals – creating new pathways, generating products and services through the utilisation of capital and intellectual capacity, and being supported by an accumulating technology base. Within this shifting structure, there is increased policing through legislation, institutions, and regulations, and sometimes through self-regulation. As Figure 2.2 shows, the corners of the marketplace are defined by technology, knowledge, and intellectual capabilities, and held in place through a legal or regulatory system. The main participants are not necessarily independent of these contours. Governments are major users and suppliers of data, while at the same time having an important role in legislation, institutional design and management, and enforcing regulations. They may also be involved in technology deepening through their efforts in public sector research and development, as well as through their role as guardians of national security and the public interest. Private entities are also users and suppliers of data with a dominant capacity for technology development entwined with skills creation and knowledge expansion in different fields. Meanwhile, individuals become active participants in this process by providing their intellectual and creative capacities to sustain the market while at the same time using technology to access and interact with service providers such as governments and private entities.

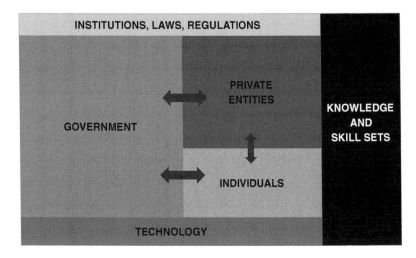

Figure 2.2 An outline of the data economy
Note: The arrows indicate data flows
Source: Authors

The complexity of data

As discussed earlier, data is now collected in various forms. These include digital, analogue, textual, visual, and aural types of data. While the sensors for collecting, transmitting, and storing them are now common, the more difficult task is to structure the data for appropriate analytics. This can be a tedious and often complicated task. Structuring and curating digital and textual data, however, can now be more readily done. The use of algorithms and machine learning capabilities has expedited this process significantly. Visual data, meanwhile, is increasingly being structured for analysis through AI, as is aural data using voice recognition technology. As deep learning improves and machines become more "intelligent," even these forms of data will become amenable to easier analysis. Thus, each sector or industry may have a variety of data forms that need to be captured and analysed. There is a significant volume and variety of data being collected, not all of which is being used for analytics. This is understandable given that there is a tendency to collect more than is required for decision-making.

As described by one author,[6] the style of data can be of different forms – large volume, unstructured, continuous flow, and of multiple formats. These data sets can also be obtained through different sources such as online, video, sensors, genomic, and the like. Different industries will obtain their data from these sources, and they may be of use in specific functional areas within the industry or the firm. For example, the supply chain function within a firm in manufacturing may obtain sensor-driven data in multiple formats, say digital and text. This data then has to be filtered, cleaned, and structured for analysis. Equally important is an ability to store the data and to curate it for further use at different times. This is now known as datafication and is an integral part of the process of converting different types of data into a form in which it can be efficiently stored, retrieved for analysis, and then curated for subsequent use. There is an array of technology that is called upon to perform these tasks, which includes remote or digital sensing, transmission, computing, and storage, all of which are managed through appropriate software capabilities. It is the integration of hardware with software that allows datafication to become a reality. In agriculture, for example, sensors dragged along by a tractor can probe the earth's electromagnetic fields to map the depth, clay content, nitrogen, and salinity of the soil to allow farmers to plant, fertilise, and water their crops with greater precision.[7]

The collection of complex data from various sources has been made possible by the advent of small and ubiquitous sensors together with the Internet of things (IoT). These sensors could be for industrial purposes such as on jet engines and turbines, or even personal use such as fitness wristbands or mobile phones using Wi-Fi and global positioning systems (GPS). Companies such as General Electric already have their own "industrial Internet" through which digital copies of their products such as jet engines, turbines, and locomotives are created and maintained.[8] The sensors on these machines send a steady stream of data to their engineers so that engine performance can be monitored and managed while maintenance routines can be tailored to each machine. There are significant cost savings to be had by these proactive methods of industrial intervention.

Big data and analytics have now, as a result, become common features in several sectors. Healthcare, airlines, financial services, travel, transportation, logistics, retail, and manufacturing are all large users of big data. This is being complemented by individuals using Internet-based services and social networks, which together provide a significant cache of data for vendors, service providers, and other entities. Meanwhile, many governments have also moved towards e-services in public administration and citizen support programmes. The Internet, without doubt, has become a facilitator for these services. Retailing is one of the more visible aspects of the data economy as more consumers use online purchasing of goods and services. However, the concomitant effect is on financial services, as most online transactions require credit or debit cards to complete the purchase.

As a result, financial service transactions have ballooned in recent years. This coalescence of different suppliers and users of data has led to significant growth in data generation.

One source[9] suggests that the largest component of data will be from cloud services, followed by that which is enterprise managed and enterprise created. The global market[10] for data is also expected to exceed 73 zetabytes by 2020, expanding from over 16 ZB in 2015. The need for storage, curation, and data management will become more urgent by then. Meanwhile, the number of connectable "things" will increase from 187 billion in 2013 to over 217 billion by 2020.[11] However, only 15% of these "things" are expected to be connected to the Internet by then, leaving a large proportion unconnected.[12]

The growth in data and the analytics that accompany it will, as a result, have a significant impact on digital intermediation. The opportunities for better data extraction and analysis will affect and improve the performance of future transactions. This may happen as predictive analytics becomes a feature of the decision-making process. It will also allow customisation of data transactions at the individual level so that tailored products or services can be offered to individuals based on their buying or other preferences. Much of this profile of the individual would have been culled and refined through algorithms combing through the data sets emanating from a social network or customer base. These changes will allow for new forms of contract to emerge as the observability between the principal and agent improves and more information adds to the efficiency of the contract.[13] Thus, the knowledge extracted from big data becomes an economic asset similar to a factor of production such as labour, capital, and technology. This will have an impact on processes, new product and service development, and the redesign of organisational structures.[14] Several challenges need to be addressed in the near-term as these features of big data become more pervasive. These include the ability to analyse and interpret unstructured data and, equally important, the conversion of these interpretations into knowledge that can add economic value to transactions. And this will depend to an extent on how the market is being reconfigured.

Reconfiguring the market

The marketplace in the production and use of data is large and is becoming more crowded. While the participants – governments, private entities, and individuals – continue to generate and use data, there is a rising class of special firms that work with data and create value. The headline companies such as Google, Amazon, Facebook, and Twitter are well known, as are

Open data sources

Government, international organisations, others

Aggregators

Marketing companies

Service providers and platform managers

Facebook, Twitter, Google, etc.

Data protectors and privacy managers

Personal data lockers

Figure 2.3 Categorisation of market participants
Source: Authors

others such as Apple, Microsoft, and IBM. These are the huge entities that undergird the world of big data. But there are several others of significance in this wide data space. Some are large, but many are smaller companies that fill niche areas such as in data aggregation and data analytics. In the main, there are four categories of these market participants, as shown in Figure 2.3. First, there are open data providers such as governments, international agencies, and private entities. While these are the more visible aspects of the data space, there is the category of highly specialised companies that provide important data services such as storage, analytics support, and data security to other market participants for a fee, with the revenues derived being shared between them and the participants. Most of the service providers are the well-known headline companies, but the category of Internet service providers (ISPs) could also be considered a part of this segment.

Second, the explosion of data has meant that market participants have a confusing array of choices in their search for specific information. This has led to a rapid growth in data aggregators. These are companies that filter and provide a selection of data sets tailored to the participant's specific requirements. The well-known ones such as TripAdvisor for hotels and Skyscanner for airline bookings are now common names. But there are similar aggregators for different industry sectors, as shown in Figure 2.4. Low entry barriers and low transaction costs have allowed these new

---

Google
Bing
TripAdvisor
Skyscanner
Zuji
Booking.com
Hotels.com

Figure 2.4 Data aggregators – examples
Source: Authors

Cloudera
Amazon Web Services
Oracle
SAP
HP
Microsoft

Figure 2.5 Data analytics providers – examples
Source: Authors

companies to emerge and become pivotal in their individual sectors. Most derive their revenues from a combination of a percentage of the booking or service charges through their websites and the advertisements that they carry.

Third, just as there has been a proliferation of aggregators, there has also been a flowering of specialised companies providing high value-added data analytics capabilities. The mainstream players are already in this space, but there are many others with unique capabilities catering to a spectrum of other participants in the data marketplace, as shown in Figure 2.5. As can be seen, former hardware manufacturers have been quick to enter this space, operating alongside the other giants. These include the likes of Hewlett-Packard and IBM.

These categories of participants provide a snapshot of how the marketplace has emerged. This may only be a temporary feature. Both technology and market demands may cause this structure to fragment as new entrants carve out specialised areas for themselves. In some instances, this is already happening, as in the insurance industry, where the linkage between medical practice, health insurance, and the travel industry is being designed, developed, and crystallised.[15] It would therefore seem that the current market structure for data is in a process of change as new entrants take advantage of technology and either bypass existing participants or link them together into a new configuration of service providers.

Fourth, and finally, there is an emerging class of specialists who provide data protection capabilities. These are companies that act as vaults, or data lockers, for storing individual profiles, which they may then sell to other companies through a revenue-sharing agreement with the individuals.

The expanding market

The data market continues to expand rapidly. The use of big data and analytics through the industrial Internet was highlighted previously. The penetration of data capture and analytics is also happening at a significant pace within manufacturing, where smart manufacturing has now become a feature of the industrial landscape. Even in this sector, however, changes are taking place rapidly as technologies that allow for 3D printing become more common.

Smart manufacturing, at its heart, involves embedding knowledge and intelligence into the actual facilities of the factory floor by collecting data, analysing it, and improving operations through the knowledge gained from the analysed data.[16] Data collection is often automated and obtained from sensors, video feeds, and digital methods, among others. This collected data forms a repository of the operations and, when analysed, can be used for both predictive and preventative measures. More specifically, this knowledge is spread horizontally across the entire organisation, with a multidisciplinary workforce able to handle a variety of tasks rather than through a narrow specialisation in one area of work. As a result of these changes on the factory floor, there are demands on the IT department to become responsive to data-intensive, real-time technologies such as IoT sensors and big data analytics. In keeping with this trend, the organisational structure of both the factory floor and the IT department is being reconfigured to adapt to smart manufacturing. This will change even further when 3D printing becomes an established feature of the manufacturing process and when full automation with made-to-measure capabilities become common.[17] Thus, the use of data analytics in automated manufacturing is already a reality and will expand further as intelligent automation becomes prevalent.

Table 2.1 Estimated size of the personal data market in Singapore (2015)

No. of relationships per household or individual	Type of relationship	No. of households or individuals (million)	Total no. of relationships (million)	Cost per relationship (S$)	Total (S$ million)
20	Household	1.23	12.3	8	196.8
45	Personal	2.46	110.7	8	885.6
65	–	–	123	–	1082.4

Source: Authors' estimates based on household data from the statistics for Singapore of 2016. Assumes an exchange rate of S$2.00 to GBP 1.00

Perhaps the more unusual expansion of the data marketplace is the creation of a market for personal data with new business models. This is a major shift in how data is shared between the individual and the market. It provides information as a tool in the hands of the individual and allows him or her to manage their relationships with many suppliers.[18] Individuals may choose to voluntarily provide information to a particular company that then sells such profiles to other companies, and the individual may then get a portion of the revenues generated by such sales through different payment modes. These could include an annual fee for access to the customer, payment per transaction, a consumer subscription that is offset against commission, and a direct consumer payment for the service.[19] There may arise other business models as these services become widespread in the future. As an example, a metric used to ascertain the size of the UK personal data market showed a direct estimated value of GBP 11.5 billion in 2014, with a further indirect revenue of around GBP 5 billion.[20] Applying the same methodology to the Singapore market, it would appear that the size of the personal data market would have been around S$1.1 billion in 2015, as shown in Table 2.1.

Regulating the market

The proliferation of data and its availability to a wide constituency also raises several issues related to privacy, confidentiality, and security. The Internet and data transactions of various forms have made it essential that personal data protection is rigorously maintained in this new data-intensive environment. Online transactions requiring financial and personal details can often be breached by those with malicious intent, which can cause significant harm to individuals, private entities, and governments. For much of the last two decades, there was self-regulation by the large private entities to ensure that such breaches did not occur. But this has been found to

An outline of the data economy 19

be insufficient to prevent breaches, and there is now legislation covering personal data protection in many countries.

Companies have, in the main, used online information to improve the accuracy of their marketing efforts and to improve customer satisfaction. It also allows them to improve their operational efficiency. Financial firms, for example, use this data for predictive analysis of credit risk. But in doing so, many of them invade the private space of individuals. While there may not be a malicious purpose behind these intrusions, they inevitably encroach upon the vulnerability of the individual consumer in different ways. If the data is not adequately anonymised, it may identify the individual in particular or provide access to personal preferences that the individual would prefer to keep confidential. The personal data protection legislation in different countries, therefore, seeks to ensure that such data is only used with the permission of the individual, and then again only for the purpose for which it has been obtained, and kept only for a reasonable period of time. In the UK, the Data Protection Act 1988, Schedule 1, provides the principles under which the legislation is operable.[21] The European Union also has a new regulation on the protection of individuals in the processing and free movement of such data.[22] In Asia, Hong Kong has the Personal Data (Privacy) Ordinance (Cap. 486), which specifies the principles under which the ordinance operates,[23] while Singapore has a Personal Data Protection Act (2012) with accompanying regulations and other subsidiary legislation to buttress the law.[24] Other countries in the region such as Japan, Korea, Australia, and New Zealand also have their own data protection laws.[25]

The fact that many, if not all, countries have legislation to protect personal data is indicative of how important this has become in recent years. More so, many also have privacy commissioners or agencies dedicated to ensuring that the penalties are enforced when there are breaches or abuses of the privacy laws. Beyond privacy laws and regulations, there are also other protections being provided through contract law, for example, or laws relating to cybersecurity, as well as the Official Secrets Act (OSA) that is effective in most Commonwealth jurisdictions.

The challenge, however, is that technology is progressing so rapidly that public understanding, policies, and laws are lagging behind this change. This is also accompanied by issues related to the definition of data that identifies a person.[26] Perhaps the more egregious concern relates to how different data streams can be combined to identify specific individuals through sophisticated algorithms. These data sets could be from social networks such as Facebook, public records, purchasing behaviour on websites, web browsing histories, and so on. More damaging could be the decisions made by algorithms that have used outdated data sets or by the assumptions that underlie the analytics. It is because of these possibilities that the various data protection laws attempt to empower individuals to possess their own data, control its use, and destroy or distribute it as they see fit.[27] But, equally, it has also been suggested that the controls on data should be imposed on data users rather than on individuals, in order to ensure that safeguards are maintained.[28]

The technology contours

The true enabler of data as a usable commodity is technology in at least three modes – hardware, operating software, and applications. The advent of cloud computing, fast communication channels such as fibre optics and wireless transmission, ever faster computer chips, the operability of the Internet, and miniaturisation of sensors have all contributed to making data more valuable and readily available. These are the innovations in hardware that have been at the forefront of how data can be collected, collated, analysed, stored, and reused.

Factory automation and smart machines depend on electronic wizardry and new materials for robotics to make them feasible. Industrial robots and automation have become a common feature in manufacturing, displacing labour in many sectors. It is forecast that more than 1.9 million industrial robots will be installed across the world by 2019, totalling over 2.6 million by that date.[29] The main users of industrial robots today are in the automotive, electrical and electronics, and machinery sectors.[30] This space will expand as robotics becomes an integral part of the labour–capital mix in industry. But the labour component in this new mix will be of a knowledge-intensive and high-skilled variety. Factory automation with robotics has increased productivity in several Organisation for Economic Co-operation and Development (OECD) countries according to a report[31] referred to by the International Federation of Robotics. Programmable robots learn and scale their learning across the factory floor and with other plants in different parts of the world, thereby improving efficiency and productivity throughout the corporation. More importantly, the cost efficiency attained through automation allows factories to reshore in the home countries rather than be located offshore in other countries. These robots and automated factories produce and use vast amounts of data, allowing remote research and development centres to program and reprogram robots from afar and use machine learning to improve the operations on the factory floor without having to be within the factory itself. Data has thus become the essential ingredient in ensuring that factory automation and robots work efficiently and without systems failures.

Automation, meanwhile, has already arrived in the service industry, and with a rapidity that is astounding. The world of automatic teller machines

(ATMs) has been in existence for more than four decades. This is being added to with newer machines that can read and accept cheques, print statements, update passbooks, and a whole host of other services that would have required manual counter services in the past. The impact of this change is widening as retail outlets, supermarkets, and restaurants switch to automated self-checkouts, menu selecting screens, and, in a twist, fully automated kitchens with few staff.[32]

The engine that allows these transformations to take place is the software that drives the equipment, whether it is a factory robot or a self-checkout terminal. Software developers in mainstream companies such as Microsoft, Apple, or IBM are being complemented by a slew of others in smaller companies specialising in different sectors. Many of these entrants bring with them open-source programs that others around the world can adapt, improve, and re-engineer. There is a catalysing effect in software development as these improvements become embedded within the software platforms that are in operation. More significantly, as data from various hardware installations become aggregated, they can be filtered and sorted through algorithms that highlight important patterns and trends. Furthermore, these analytic techniques facilitate inventive reuses of data.[33] While in the past this required the hand, and mind, of a trained programmer, this can now be done through computers that learn from patterns and improve the software on their own. This "deep learning" or "AI" has had a profound effect on the speed with which software enhancements can be tested and implemented. As a result, algorithms and coding that were once the preserve of programmers have now become a part of the intelligent literacy of machines. This change in the labour–capital mix has had a dramatic impact on how services are delivered, as lead times have shortened considerably. More importantly, machine learning makes it possible for data delivery to be hermetic with little or no human intervention.

While machine learning and software development go hand in hand, another group of creative individuals is involved in developing various applications that are supported by the operating platforms in place. The use of mobile phones to run these applications, ranging from controlling household air-conditioning and temperature, observing traffic density on the highways, flying drones, and a host of other possibilities, is now common. Some of these applications have drawn their inspiration from computer games, others from a discerned need in the marketplace. Many of these have had social benefits that have far exceeded their developers' original expectations. Examples of these are the M-Pesa money transfer system through mobile phones widely used in Africa, the weather reports and commodity prices on mobile phones for farmers in India, and mobile phone-based disaster warnings in remote places in Indonesia. The applications world is growing at a fast pace, with new offerings being presented every day or so. The confluence of these three major streams – hardware, operating software, and applications – has provided a vast and rich universe of data sets. The collected data has also become more valuable as algorithms extract key information for decision-making. As interconnectivity increases through the IoT and mobile communications become more efficient, such as through 4G, the amount of data will grow even more rapidly. This global growth in data and analytics is forecast to generate around USD 187 billion in revenues by 2019.[34] But technology itself often requires the intervention of the human mind to become intelligent and "human-like." And as machine learning takes hold, the need for very specialised skills and knowledge grows in tandem. There is also an intensity to how these features become a part of the data economy.

Knowledge and skills

The design of algorithms, coding of programs, and managing data systems requires scientific and engineering skills. These are knowledge-intensive in nature and require long years of education in science, mathematics, and, in some instances, humanities. The unusual feature of the new knowledge needed in analysing data is that it has a core of scientific thinking with a periphery of other types of knowledge such as language and linguistics. This should not be surprising given that data in textual, visual, and aural forms requires a facility in these humanistic areas for their analysis and interpretation. It is the unstructured form of data that demands such intervention. Structured data obtained from sensors and machines are mostly already digital and can be easily analysed. But the combination of structured and unstructured data for a particular service or industry requires complex capabilities that draw upon teams of specialists to design algorithms and to code programs. This has led to the emergence of a new type of computer-based skill in a field called data science.

Data science encompasses a spectrum of activities, as shown in Figure 2.6. There is the stage of data generation and acquisition that feeds into data analysis and processing. This then moves to storage and curation before ending with valuation and usage. It is in the analysis and processing stage that algorithms are designed and implemented. Areas such as semantic analysis require more than just quantitative skills.

Beyond data analysis and processing, there is a need for storing and curating the data. This is a time-consuming and intensive task that prepares data for further detailed use in modelling and predictive analysis. The final stage of data valuation and usage draws upon knowledge of statistics, optimisation techniques, simulation and forecasting, and several other

1. Data acquisition capability
   a. Structured and unstructured data
   b. Sensors
   c. Video feeds
2. Data analysis and processing skills
   a. Pre-processing
   b. Correlations
   c. Pattern recognition
   d. Semantic analysis
   e. Machine learning
3. Data storage, curation, and management
   a. Storage
   b. Data augmentation and annotation
   c. Validation
   d. Consistency analysis
   e. No/new Structured Query Language
   f. Revision and updates
4. Data value creation through applications
   a. Modelling
   b. Decision support
   c. Simulation
   d. Predictive analytics
5. Cybersecurity and privacy protection
   a. Data protection
   b. Privacy management
   c. Trust creation and maintenance

Figure 2.6 The skills spectrum in data science
Source: Authors

mathematical methods. Taken as a whole, the data scientist is expected to be familiar with a wide spectrum of activities. The demand on the data scientist is not just in computing and mathematics, but also in pattern recognition and visualising data. However, with more frequent use of machine learning techniques, there are now ready-to-install, off-the-shelf algorithms that can shorten the time taken for data analytics. Much of the analytics and statistical modelling can also now be done through distributed processing and cloud computing, allowing for more efficient analysis. A consequence of this development is that data scientists can now specialise in one or more areas of the spectrum, rather than being expected to be knowledge-able in all areas. Recent research has shown that 60% of the data scientist's time is spent on cleaning and organising data and a further 19% is spent on collecting data sets.[35] The remainder of their time is spent on mining data for patterns, refining algorithms, building training sets, and performing other activities.[36] These different functions in a corporate setting have led to the creation of a chief data scientist who will be responsible for managing machine learning capabilities, designing algorithms, and supporting more accurate financial reporting through the analytics on data.[37] Beyond the skills for the direct tasks in the data science spectrum, there is the continuous need for data security, data protection, privacy, and maintenance of trust. A category of specialists in these areas is now common, as hackers and others can try to break into secure systems, resulting in data loss, ransom demands, and locked-out systems. In the context of trust and privacy, there is also a growing need for lawyers knowledgeable in the law relating to data privacy and cybersecurity.

When the skill sets are disaggregated and reconstituted, five critical functions with specific knowledge areas can be observed as being important in data science, as given in Table 2.2.

While knowledge in these technical areas is a given, there are two other areas in which the data scientist is expected to be adept. These are in framing decisions by acting as an advisor on the types of analytics to be done and communicating these in an understandable manner to others in the corporate hierarchy at one level and being able to understand the business and its demands so that the outputs can be tailored to the requirements of strategy, finance, and operations at another. The challenge is that it is often unusual for the technically fluent to operate in these two other areas with a high level of competency. The demands on data scientists are therefore onerous. This is made all the more difficult when it is seen that even as data is expected to grow rapidly, there is already a shortage of data scientists.[38] Meanwhile, the median salaries for data scientists now range from USD

Table 2.2 Functional knowledge in data science

Technical	Quantitative	Strategy	Applications
Coding	Analytics	Decision framing	Business applications
Data architecture	Statistical analysis	Advisory services	Marketing
Technology use	Visual analytics	Communications	Product design
	Machine learning	Process design	
	Data interpretation		

Source: Authors

91,000 for juniors to around USD 250,000 for senior managers.[39] There is, in the meantime, a scramble to produce more data scientists as universities rush to set up data science programmes and companies introduce in-house training programmes to fill the gap.

Fitting the pieces together

This chapter has outlined the various elements that, when assembled, make up the data economy. As can be seen, the marketplace for data is growing and becoming more complex. Structured and unstructured data have become more common, with several streams of unstructured data becoming available through visual, textual, and sometimes audio technologies. This poses a challenge for data scientists as they develop algorithms to decipher the data and structure it for further analysis. All participants – governments, private entities, individuals – in the data marketplace have become producers and users of data through digital and other means. The proliferation of data and its use has now made it a valuable commodity for governments, companies, and individuals.

Value is being created by analysing data for its underlying patterns and drawing important insights. While business-to-business data transactions are more readily amenable to different forms of valuation based on the usefulness (or otherwise) of the data, the difficulty is in valuing personal data. Different models of personal data valuation have been suggested.[40] These include net income per individual record, costs of a data breach, market prices for the offer and purchase of personal data, economic experiments and surveys, and insurance costs to protect data.

Meanwhile, the technology frontier is expanding at a remarkable pace, leaving the legal and policy environments behind. The changing technology contours have allowed for more efficient data transmission, faster processing, and enhanced machine learning capabilities. Taken together, these features have made data analytics an inseparable part of government and business. In particular, business operations and market strategies have become more robust and targeted at specific customer segments in many cases, while at the same time improving operational efficiency in other ways. For individuals, the change in technology has allowed for better access to applications, improved business services, and more secure personal communications.

The increased availability of data and its uses also raise concerns over data privacy and protection of the individual. Almost all countries now have data protection legislation to prevent the misuse of data and the causing of harm to the individual. But technology has also provided other ways of protecting privacy through algorithms that can anonymise data and through newer statistical techniques known as differential privacy, which can inject neat clones into the data sets to prevent identification of the individual. Nonetheless, the hand of the government to legislate and protect the individual and private parties has also had to be strengthened in the light of the profusion of data in daily life.

A feature of the explosion in data is the emergence of specialist firms that connect with the major players in the sector at one level and compete at another. These are firms that provide data aggregation, data analytics, data protection and cybersecurity, and a host of other niche services. The marketplace for data services is now complex and crowded. Low entry barriers and low transaction costs have been boons for this flowering of a new class of high value-added services.

The effect of a proliferation of these companies alongside the mainstream corporates such as Google, Amazon, IBM, and Facebook is the emergence of a value chain within the data science marketplace. This has led to the need for different skills and the emergence of data scientists. The knowledge and skill sets of data scientists have become exacting and, in the broader sense, require an "artistic" touch. These other artistic facets expected of data scientists include in-house advisory services and becoming a member of the supporting cast for the likes of the strategy and operations pundits. In some cases, the designation of chief data scientist implies strategic leadership within corporates that see data as a valuable commodity. There is, in the meantime, a shortage of data scientists and, no doubt, an even bigger shortage of data science leaders in the corporate world.

The challenge of cultures

The use of data analytics for decision-making brings with it several challenges. Many are technical and can be addressed with some ingenuity. But the more difficult concern is that of the conflict between digital culture and its overall environment. The use of algorithms for data extraction and analysis is seldom understood by the non-specialist. There is always the fear that an unknown or unknowable process is being used to define outcomes over which there is little human control. This is a valid concern, and data scientists have become aware of the need to make their processes and mathematical techniques transparent. Nonetheless, gross suspicions still prevail in the manner in which data is collected and analysed.

The more apparent issue is the way in which data is collected and then curated and used. There are issues related to privacy of the individual and the way in which data exhaust is then utilised for purposes other than for which the original data was collected. This is an important concern, and redrawn legislation in many countries attempts to address it. The right to be forgotten on the databases when the use of the data is complete, the requirement for consent in the collection and use of data, and other specific requirements are now part of the wider discourse in data collection and, by extension, in the ensuing analytics. The need to engage citizens in a more conciliatory fashion and the need to obtain a higher quality of data are the drivers of a data-driven strategy for better municipal decision-making. Examples of these include better road maintenance, traffic reports, garbage disposal, and environmental controls.[41]

While these are the external concerns of citizens and customers in how personal data is being used, a more intense organisation culture debate is taking place within corporations and government agencies. Here, the issue is how best to build a new culture of management in a digital (and data-driven) environment for sustained growth. Several management methods[42] have been suggested to address this emerging issue. These include greater delegation, a risk-taking culture, and a more action-orientated organisation with collaboration amongst teams. This is not a new development, however. Such approaches have been common in the research and development industry, but they become important in the data-driven economy, driving features for corporate growth.

Both of these concerns – the internal organisational and the external public interface – raise the need for a digitally literate community to become participants in a data-intensive environment. There are two compelling narratives that bridge this challenge. The first is the generation that has been brought up in the world of digital products. These are the millennials who have a familiarity with and a capability to participate with little or no difficulty in the digitised data world. They use their smartphones, tablets, and laptops to interact in a variety of ways with public services and commercial activities such as banking, payments, and the like. The second are those from the earlier generations who have no familiarity with digital products and for whom there is a steep learning process in their use. They require simple digital and data-driven products and a heavy dose of digital education to bring them into the data-driven economy. The need to therefore bridge the "digital divide" has become all the more significant in the new data economy.

The context of this study

This study is aimed at how a data economy is being created in a city-state such as Singapore that has been aggressively promoting its capabilities as an important node for applied analytics. Several international companies have set up centres in the city for consumer analytics, data analytics for urban planning, data mining, traffic management, and high-performance computing, amongst others.[43] This is being further augmented by an ambitious drive to ensure that data analytics will contribute around S$1 billion in value to gross domestic product (GDP) in 2017, and also to become the compelling location for proprietary banking services.[44] Meanwhile, local universities are offering several data analytics courses to prepare data scientists for the new economy. In effect, many of the features of a data economy are already present in Singapore. The challenge, as elsewhere, will be to extract the context of how data is being used and how to value it in a meaningful manner.

In order to gauge how data can be a transforming feature of the economy and how it can be used for decision-making, this study looks at data from the transportation sector in Singapore. It seeks to identify important value-generating possibilities and outline the legal and regulatory environment in which data and individuals are protected. It also studies the process of obtaining data and structuring it for analysis in the context of handling public and private data sources. And this forms the rubric of the following chapter.

Notes

1 *The Economist*, 6 May 2017.
2 Mayer-Schonberger, Viktor and Kenneth Cuiker, *Big Data: A Revolution That Will Transform How We Live, Work, and Think*, John Murray, London, 2013, pp. 83–84.
3 Sousa, Sonia, "How Should the Government Approach the Big Data Challenge?" Big Innovation Centre, Lancaster University, 2013.
4 R.H. Coase, "The Nature of the Firm," *Economica*, 1937, 4:386–405.
5 Tapscott, Don, *The Digital Economy*, McGraw Hill, New York, 2015.
6 Davenport, Thomas, *Big Data @ Work*, HBR Press, Boston, MA, 2014.
7 Lohr, Steve, *Data-ism: Inside the Big Data Revolution*, Oneworld, London, 2016, pp. 126–127.
8 *Ibid.*, pp. 140–142.
9 CSC.com
10 *Ibid.*
11 IDC, 2014.
12 *Ibid.*
13 H. Varian, "Computer Mediated Transactions," *American Economic Review*, 2010, 100:1–10.
14 Sousa, Sonia. "How Should the Government Approach the Big Data Challenge?" Big Innovation Centre, Lancaster University, 2013.
15 Author's own work on the "insuretech" industry in New Zealand and Australia.
16 P. O'Donovan, K. Leahy, K. Bruton, & D.T.J. O'Sullivan, "An industrial big data pipeline for data-driven analytics maintenance applications in large-scale manufacturing facilities," *Journal of Big Data*, 2015, 2:25.

17 Ford, Martin, *Rise of the Robots,* Basic Books, New York, 2015, p. 10.
18 Ctrl-Shift, "Personal Information Management Systems: An Analysis of an Emerging Market," www.ctrl-shift.co.uk, June 2014.
19 *Ibid.*
20 *Ibid.*
21 Data Protection Act 1988, legislation.gov.uk.
22 EU General Data Protection Regulation, eur-lex.europa.eu.
23 Personal Data (Privacy) Ordinance (Cap. 486), pcpd.org.hk.
24 Personal Data Protection Act 2012, statutes.agc.gov.sg.
25 Privacy Act 1988 in Australia; Privacy Act 1993 in New Zealand; Act on the Protection of Personal Information (Amended) 2016 in Japan; Personal Information Protection Act (Amended) 2015 in Korea.
26 Lohr, Steve, *op. cit.*, p. 187.
27 Lohr, Steve, *op. cit.*, p. 204.
28 Mayer-Schonberger, *op. cit.*, p. 193.
29 International Federation of Robotics, ifr.org, 29 September 2016.
30 *Ibid.*
31 Centre for Economics Research and Business, 2017.
32 Ford, *op. cit.*, p. 14.
33 Franks, Bill, *The Analytics Revolution,* Wiley, Hoboken, NJ, 2014.
34 IDC, idc.com, 23 May 2016.
35 CrowdFlower 2016, as given in raconteur, raconteur.net, October 2016.
36 *Ibid.*
37 *Ibid.*
38 It is estimated that the USA will have a shortage of 190,000 data scientists by 2018 according to McKinsey Global Institute, 2013.
39 Forbes, 2015.
40 OECD, "Exploring the Economics or Personal Data: A Survey of Methodologies for Measuring Monetary Value," OECD Digital Economy Papers, No. 220, OECD Publishing, Paris.
41 Authors' findings from interviews in the Smart City Hub in Jakarta, 2018.
42 Hemering, Kilman, et al., "Its Not a Digital Transformation without a Digital Culture," Boston Consulting Group, 13 April 2018.
43 Economic Development Board, as given in Harvard Business Review Analytic Report 2014.
44 *Ibid.*

3   The search for data

Data is often viewed as a by-product or as a cost to be minimised. With increasing digitisation and greater interconnectivity through networks, the cost of data has dramatically decreased even while the quality of data has increased substantially. It has now reached a point that data is no longer a costly by-product, but an economically viable asset to be gathered, nurtured, and harvested.

Businesses were the first to see data as a gold mine. Companies such as Google and Facebook understood the commercial value of data and developed successful business models that thrive spectacularly on having data in hand. Other companies – even those for which data is far from central in their activities – are beginning to realise that the seemingly useless data generated by other processes can have unexploited business value, sometimes in rather indirect ways. For example, telecommunication companies collect massive amounts of operational data from call detail records and mobile phone usage. These data sets can be mined for a wealth of deep insights about their customers' behaviour, preferences, movements, and activities, sometimes even as they happen, in real time. Such knowledge can provide communications services providers and others with unprecedented competitive advantages and create new revenue streams and business opportunities.[1]

Governments were the next to see the usefulness of data. With a smart city infrastructure that collects data from the environment, transportation, public utility, buildings, and so on, cities have become big generators of data. This data provides new opportunities for understanding the city and its people better. Open government data initiatives such as data.gov and data.gov.uk that were launched in 2009 as transformative government services for transparency and policy innovation have been enthusiastically adopted by many cities worldwide[2] and have resulted in a wealth of data sets collected by public agencies being made available to the public through online portals. This approach has provided a new platform for governments to engage and collaborate with their citizens and businesses to deliver better public services, which could ultimately translate into creating economic value. The availability of government data also allows citizens to be active in identifying and resolving issues themselves.

In this increasingly data-centric social and economic landscape, shaped by a hyper-connected world with widespread adoption of advanced intelligent information and communication technologies, data is expected to become the focus of the future knowledge economy and society. What are the promising economic and social opportunities for both the private and public sectors? Are there new policy implications arising from the proliferation of data as a kind of economic asset? And what are the key technological considerations for shaping this future data economy into a prosperous one for businesses while also safeguarding citizens' interests?

To seek answers to these important questions, this study has focused on an analytics case with the following criteria:

- It should have an emerging footprint in big data and an important role in the economy, without an apparent interconnection between the two;
- The real data should be obtained with some ease;
- A feasible technical solution with the data can be implemented; and
- It has a sufficient perimeter to highlight the legal and governance concerns that attend it.

Singapore was chosen as the case study with data drawn from its transportation system for several reasons. The most important determinant was the fact that the funding agency for the research, the National Research Foundation, was seeking a Singapore-centred research agenda. Further, Singapore has been at the forefront of using big data and analytics for several public sector services in recent years. The implementation of a Smart Nation programme accelerated many of these projects. The fully integrated bus and rail transportation system is also a repository of vast amounts data being analysed through various algorithms to improve operating efficiency and managing the network. These data sets were made readily available to the study team. While Singapore was thus selected as the case study, the team also did comparative evaluations of other cities in the region. This was largely in the context of the legislative and regulatory environments that defined the use of data in these jurisdictions.

Singapore, the Smart Nation

Singapore announced its Smart Nation initiative[3] in 2014 to "harness the power of networks, data and infocomm technologies to improve living, create economic opportunity and build a closer community." In 2017, Singapore was ranked the top performer in the global smart city performance ranking study by Juniper Research, sponsored by Intel.[4] Of the cities studied, Singapore came out tops in all of the key areas measured, namely mobility, healthcare, public safety, and productivity.

Singapore did not become a smart nation overnight. The Singapore government had long demonstrated great foresight in its vision for information technology and its role in the country's economic development. Back in the 1980s, when there were "only some 400 computer users in Singapore," the government had already foreseen that computers would "soon be a common feature in offices, factories, schools and the home."[5] Its journey to become a smart nation started as early as 1981 with the formation of the National Computer Board (NCB) and the launch of the Civil Service Computerisation Programme soon after the board was set up. This was followed by a slew of well-planned and ambitious initiatives over several decades, such as the National Computerisation Plan (1981–1985), the National IT Plan (1986–1991), IT2000 (1992–1999), Infocomm 21 (2000–2003), Connected Singapore (2003–2006), and Intelligent Nation (2006–2015).

As Singapore prepares for its next chapter[6] as a smart nation, it has noted that data must be seen "as a new resource compared to the traditional resources like water, energy, oil and so forth,"[7] and Singapore will need to improve its ability to use it productively in the economy to leverage this increasingly important source of comparative advantage. In fact, there is a specific recommendation by the Committee on the Future Economy (CFE) in its 2017 report to "harness data as an asset" and catalyse the use of data in the economy. As such, Singapore was the natural choice for our study on the data economy.

Case: public transportation

We considered possible case studies in various data-rich sectors (e.g. healthcare, finance), and eventually decided upon a data analytics case study on *public transportation*, as this best satisfied the case criteria given earlier, and Singapore was well known for its innovations in urban mobility.

Transportation is an important component of the economy – efficient urban mobility makes effective use of the limited resources in cities and provides economic and social benefits that can result in positive multiplier effects for commerce, employment, and social interaction. As such, most cities invest heavily in good infrastructure for urban transportation.

Transportation nevertheless has also been developing a large footprint in big data in recent years. In terms of public transportation, automated fare collection (AFC) systems using smart card technologies for e-payments on public buses, subways, and trains have been widely adopted in big cities. In semi-public transportation, most cities' taxicabs and, increasingly, delivery trucks are also equipped with GPS units for fleet management and navigation. These systems generate large amounts of real-time ridership and trajectory data. These data sets can be used to understand and evaluate the dynamics of urban transportation.

Indeed, the amount, type, and quality of transportation data available will continue to improve in leaps and bounds. Other than public transportation, mobility data for private vehicles may also become available with the increased adoption of digitised payment systems for parking and advancements in next-generation satellite-based electronic road toll collection systems.[8] These payment data can be used to piece together the digital footprints of private vehicles in the city, just like the AFC systems for public transit. The advent of autonomous vehicles, which is heavily dependent on information and communication technologies, will generate fine-grained digital footprints of vehicles in the future. Furthermore, non-transit data such as call detail records and mobile phone usage collected by telecommunication companies can be used to discover user movement and activities, as highlighted earlier.

The increased abundance of rich data generated by intelligent transport and other technological systems provides information of greater granularity for building dynamic and behaviourally rich models about urban mobility. A valuable data subset begins to emerge if these new high-definition urban mobility data and their models can be used to provide insights not only to stakeholders in the transportation sector, but also to other stakeholders of the city, especially businesses, to power new economic opportunities and attain better social outcomes.

In order to develop an understanding of how the availability of these new data sources may be used to shape the future data economy and to comprehend the possible hurdles that may hinder it, this case study focuses on public transit AFC data. As stated earlier, most modern cities have adopted AFC systems to automate and manage payments for their public transit networks. With AFC systems, public transit fares are collected by an automated reader next to the driver of a bus or at a turnstile of a subway station entrance. As a passenger enters or exits a bus or a subway station, the passenger presents ("tap in" or "tap out") to the respective automated reader his or her smart card, which contains an embedded microchip for storing data about the journey. The smart card interacts in a contactless fashion with the automated reader, which is a smart device that not only reads and validates the passenger's card, but also collects the fare for the journey in accordance with specified tariffs.

Some examples of contactless smart cards used for public transit include the Oyster card in London, the Octopus card in Hong Kong, and the Suica card in Japan. In Singapore, the card that is commonly used for public transportation services – public bus services as well as mass rapid transit (MRT) and light rail transit (LRT) – is the ez-link card, issued by EZ-Link Pte Ltd, a private company established by Singapore's LTA[9] in 2002 as its wholly owned subsidiary to manage contactless payment services for public transit. Since adopting the Singapore Standard for Contactless ePurse Application (CEPAS) in 2008, EZ-Link has extended its card acceptance beyond transit to more than 30,000 points across the island state, including retail shops, food and beverage outlets, private transport, government services, and community services; as well as for electronic road pricing and at car parks fitted with the electronic payment system. According to its website,[10] EZ-Link has issued more than 17 million CEPAS-compliant ez-link cards to date, and "almost every Singaporean carries at least one ez-link card in his or her wallet."

In search of data: EZ-Link

The wide adoption of the ez-link cards by Singaporeans for public transportation payment suggests that a complete and comprehensive data set for studying urban mobility based on public transportation is available. As a consequence, EZ-Link was selected to provide such a data set.

Like many companies that possess large sets of data as a by-product and are beginning to realise that data has become a commodity in demand, EZ-Link was keen to explore and embrace potential business opportunities that may be brought forth by the data economy. A non-disclosure agreement (NDA) was signed with the company and a historical data set for a three-month duration of its ez-link card transactions was provided for analytics.

The data set was pre-anonymised by the company's own Data Protection Officer (DPO) to remove all private and sensitive information. This is in keeping with the requirements of Singapore's Personal Data Protection Act 2012 (PDPA), which requires organisations to designate at least one individual as the DPO[11] to oversee the data protection responsibilities within the organisation and ensure compliance with the PDPA.

The data set consisted of transactions that include both public transit and non-public transit spending of its ez-link customers using the smart card for cashless payments on:

- Public buses, MRT, and LRT;
- Private transport services, such as taxis and private buses;
- Electronic road pricing and electronic parking systems;
- Food and beverage outlets;
- Shopping and retail outlets;

- Leisure and entertainment outlets;
- Government services;
- Community clubs;
- Self-services such as vending machines, photocopying and photo printing services.

There were approximately an equal number of transit and non-transit transactions made between 1 January 2016 and 31 March 2016 on a total of 4.6 million ez-link cards:

- 447 million public transport transactions (about 5 million transactions per day);
- 440 million non-public transportation transactions (another 5 million per day).

Data gaps

The ez-link data set appeared rich in information at first glance. However, on closer inspection, there were numerous data gaps in the ez-link data set that made it inadequate for analysing urban mobility on its own. For example, the trip origin (tap-in) information for the subway transactions is not captured in the ez-link data set, despite the fact that passengers are required to validate their cards when entering (tap in) and exiting (tap out) the stations. Only the tap-out locations are captured by EZ-Link, as the payment transactions occur upon trip completion.

For bus journey payments, the information captured by EZ-Link has less information density. For example, although bus passengers are required to validate their ez-link cards when both boarding and alighting, the data captured by EZ-Link is payment for a generic bus journey – the bus route – while the boarding and alighting bus stops are not captured in the data set.

The ez-link data set also had little or no demographic information. Out of the 4.6 million ez-link cards, only around 230,000 (or 5%) were registered with user profiles obtained via various marketing campaigns.

For most firms, data is collected to serve their core business, and EZ-Link's core business is in the clearing and settlement of all ez-link card transactions generated in transit and non-transit (retail/merchant) environments, as well as the sale, distribution, and overall management of its ez-link cards. The data collected by EZ-Link is therefore largely focused on recording payment transactions. The traditional view of data as a cost to be minimised leads to the minimal amount of information captured.

As companies like EZ-Link will collect the minimum data needed to serve their sole business purposes, it may not be straightforward to repurpose the data collected for alternative uses to seek new economic opportunities. With the rapid progress in technology that has improved data capture, aggregation, and processing, companies embarking on a transformative journey into a data-rich environment require a rethink of their data strategy to create data assets that are rich in information in order to generate economic value for their core businesses and beyond. Only then can they widen and, in many instances, deepen knowledge of their customers and their preferences. Increasingly, this will become an important aspect of big data and analytics as firms realise the usefulness of data analytics.

In search of data: LTA

The gaps in data obtained from EZ-Link had to be overcome and the data made suitable for analytics, with the recognition that urban mobility is a complex domain with multiple stakeholders. Other than smart card managers such as EZ-Link, there are also the public transport operators, the authorities, and passengers. Furthermore, there may also be multiple players in each of these categories. For example, in cashless transit payments such as stored-value cash cards, other than EZ-Link there is also NETS[12] and an emerging number of new mobile payment players. All are active participants in the supply and use of data in one form or the other. Each company, like EZ-Link, will collect data based on its specific core business and interest, leading to possible data gaps.

As mentioned earlier, governments have also become active participants in the collection and use of data. As such, more data was sought from the main agency for public transport infrastructure and systems, the LTA.

Singapore's LTA is one of the world's most forward-thinking and tech-savvy transport regulators. Data analytics plays a key role in LTA's efforts in planning, operating, and maintaining the land transport infrastructure and systems for the city-state. In 2010, it set up an award-winning PLANET[13] (Planning for Land TrAnsport NETwork) data warehouse that can ingest up to 12 million public transport transactions per day and hold three years' worth of data and information from public transport, traffic, vehicle, and geographical information systems. PLANET enables LTA's transport planners to mine data from cross-functional data sources to validate policy assumptions and make empirical, evidence-based decisions.

LTA provided a public transit data set from its PLANET system consisting of both tap-in and tap-out information of public transit (bus, MRT, and LRT) passengers. This data set for the month of March 2016 fit with that from EZ-Link as it lay within the same time horizon of the three-month data from EZ-Link. The data set consisted of the trip information of 5.5 million public transit cards[14] with the following breakdown in terms of mode of public transit:

- For MRT and LRT, there was a total of 78 million trips, or an average of 2.5 million trips per day;
- For public buses, there was a total of 111 million trips, or an average of 3.6 million trips per day.

In terms of protection of data confidentiality, pre-anonymisation of the data was carried out by LTA's DPO, as was the case with EZ-Link. This data, coming from an agency of the government, was ruled by the OSA,[15] unlike the need for an NDA with EZ-Link. Under the OSA, the disclosure of information to unauthorised parties is an offence that is punishable by fines and imprisonment.

Data protection: de-identification limitations

Given that the data sets had been pre-anonymised, the requirements imposed upon the investigators who must agree – either personally or as an organisation – to strict legal terms and conditions (NDA for EZ-Link and OSA for LTA) for protecting data confidentiality may have seemed unnecessary. Pre-anonymisation of the data sets was done with standard de-identification techniques by removing the direct identifiers such as the CAN ID (a unique, 16-digit card ID).[16] However, the common practice of removing identifying information can be inadequate for anonymity, as there could be a set of quasi-identifiers (or indirect identifiers) in the de-identified data that can be used to uniquely re-identify different individuals.

In this case, the smart card data sets that were obtained contained human mobility data. Researchers have shown that there is a close correlation between an individual's identity and their movement patterns,[17] and a recent study on human mobility data showed that a majority of human mobility traces are uniquely identifiable given just a few random spatio-temporal points.[18]

These observations were used to develop a matching algorithm for linking the smart card records that had been independently pre-anonymised in the two data sets from EZ-Link and LTA. If we assume that $(l_1, l_2, ..., l_n)$ and $(e_1, e_2, ..., e_n)$ are the time series of n tap-out records of any two anonymised cards within the same time periods in the LTA and EZ-Link data sets, respectively, it is possible to find unique matches of $(l_1, l_2, ..., l_n)$ and $(e_1, e_2, ..., e_n)$ in the two data sets with just a small sample size, n. In other words, by using the cards' MRT station tap-out time series information to derive unique tap-out location sequence signatures, the algorithm matches the anonymised smart cards in the two data sets. Applying this technique, the study was able to derive concise, unique travel pattern signatures, namely $(l_1, l_2, ..., l_n)$ and $(e_1, e_2, ..., e_n)$, to match the anonymous commuters in the two data sets.

Although the two independently pre-anonymised data sets had their direct identifiers duly removed, the pseudo-identifiers in the data sets can be used for integrating the data sets. This also revealed a potential privacy risk of re-identification despite the pre-anonymisation of the data sets. In this case, it is possible for an attacker to deliberately collect auxiliary movement information of a target, either by actual observation or by inference from online digital traces that most people tend to share. This auxiliary information about the target can be exploited for re-identification by the attacker. For example, consider an attacker targeting a colleague who is known to commute to work by MRT. The attacker clearly knows the office location of the targeted colleague. By collecting some actual data about the colleague's times of arrival at the office for a few days, the attacker can use the auxiliary information collected to construct a movement signature that is unique enough to associate a particular smart card in the data set to the particular colleague. The re-identification becomes easier the more auxiliary information about the target the attacker is privy to, such as where the targeted colleague stays. Once a particular de-identified smart card in the data set is re-identified as belonging to the targeted colleague, the target's entire movements, besides commuting to work, can then be revealed from the data set, including where he or she visits during private hours.

In fact, it has been repeatedly shown that by taking advantage of auxiliary information, it is possible to link an individual to a record in data sets that appeared to have been protected using de-identification. In an early case in 1997, researchers showed that it was possible to re-identify prominent persons – in this particular case, Massachusetts Governor William Weld[19] – from a duly de-identified medical insurance data set using auxiliary information that could be relatively easily obtained for people with such prominence. Since then, it has become feasible to re-identify common folks in anonymised data sets in the age of big data where auxiliary information about most people can often be obtained with ease. There were numerous highly publicised cases that demonstrated that re-identification risks are not limited to prominent people, namely the cases for Netflix[20] and AOL,[21] and more recently the case of New York City taxi data.[22]

To address the issue of re-identification by pseudo-identifiers in the data, privacy researchers have endeavoured to develop stronger protection frameworks such as k-anonymity[23] with sophisticated data anonymisation algorithms based on these frameworks. The k-anonymity protection model ensures that the data for each person in a data set cannot be distinguished from at least $k - 1$ individuals whose data is also in the data set. This means that k-anonymity anonymisation algorithms guarantee that the quasi-identifiers present in the released data set appear in at least k records. In this way, an attacker is unable to tell for sure that a given person is in the data set (membership disclosure). In fact, it is also not possible to tell whether a given person has a certain sensitive attribute (sensitive attribute disclosure) or which record corresponds to a given person (identity disclosure).

To achieve k-anonymity, a typical data anonymisation technique used is *generalisation* – that is, replacing quasi-identifiers with less specific but semantically consistent values until there are at least k records with identical generalised values. Clearly, applying generalisation on the data values to achieve k-anonymity often leads to loss of information, which can significantly reduce the utility of the anonymised data set for analytics tasks. In fact, for k-anonymity to be applicable, it requires that each of the records in the original data set must have at least k close neighbours, and this is often not true in many high-dimensional, real-world data sets.[24] As such, the utility of k-anonymity in practice is limited.

Other than k-anonymity, data privacy researchers have also come up with several alternative privacy protection models such as l-diversity[25] and t-closeness.[26] However, these models have their limitations for practical adoption. Given that there is no perfect data anonymisation model to date despite the hard work of privacy researchers, it is likely that perfect anonymisation is a myth.

Nevertheless, privacy and confidentiality concerns should not be allowed to hamper access to data, which is the essential fuel for a viable data economy. Privacy researchers need to continue to research robust theoretical and operational frameworks for privacy protection that can allow adequate data utility in support of the data economy, while policy-makers must become aware of both the possibilities and limitations of privacy technologies and devise suitable legal instruments to limit the misuse of sensitive data. To effectively tackle the hard problem of data privacy, for which a perfect solution may not exist, policy-makers and researchers need to work hand-in-hand to address the technological and sociolegal considerations based on a clear understanding of the social and legal requirements, as well as the possibilities and limitations of technologies in the ever-changing landscape of big data. This will be revisited at the end of next chapter, where some of the emerging technologies that address data privacy are discussed.

Next: analysis of data

Having obtained data from different entities, there remained the challenge of seeking insights through analytics on both sets of data. The aim was to seek promising economic and social opportunities for both the private and public sectors. Table 3.1 below summarises the differences between the two data sets.

There is an important difference in the two data sets in that one data set from a private company (EZ-Link) is payment-centric, and the other from a

Table 3.1 Comparison of the EZ-Link and LTA data sets

EZ-Link	LTA
Three-month data set	One-month data set
Pre-anonymised	Pre-anonymised
NDA required between organisations	OSA required of individual team members
MRT and LRT: tap out only	MRT and LRT: tap in and tap out
Bus: payment only	Bus: tap in, tap out, route number
Included non-transit transactions	No other transactions
Some user information for registered cards	No user information except concession pass types (children and seniors)

Source: Authors; EZ-Link Pte Ltd; LTA

public agency (LTA) is trip-centric. While the commercial ez-link data set was incomplete at the trip level (no information on tap in and bus routes), it contained non-transit payment information as well as some demographic information that could be useful for discovering possible correlations between consumer and commuter behavioural patterns in the urban setting. While the LTA data set had complete trip information on public transit, it did not contain demographic information, nor other non-transit information that the ez-link data set provided. While the data sets appeared to have different parameters for their respective entities, the sharing of the data sets from EZ-Link and LTA presents an opportunity to combine the two to provide a richer information set than either one could on its own. Given that the data sets had a common time period and horizon (i.e. a one-month intersection between the two data sets in March 2016), they could be merged using the re-identification technique as described above. The next chapter looks at the analysis of the combined data sets in greater detail.

Notes

1 For example, the leading telecommunication company in Singapore – Singtel – has created a new company called DataSpark in 2014 to offer geoanalytics and consumer research services based on data sourced from Singtel's mobile telecommunications network.
2 Including Singapore: data.gov.sg.
3 www.smartnation.sg/happenings/speeches/smart-nation-launch.
4 "Smart Cities – What's in It for Citizens?", Juniper Research, March 2018.
5 "Developing Singapore as a Software Centre – A Second Report." Speech by Dr Tony Tan at the Opening Ceremony of Applications 83/Computa 83, World Trade Centre Exhibition Hall 3, 11 May 1983.

6   Singapore celebrated its first 50 years of nation building in 2015.

7   www.gov.sg/news/content/channel-newsasia-data-could-give-singapore-a-competitive-advantage-chan-chun-sing.

8   For example, Singapore – the first city to implement automated electronic road toll collection for congestion pricing using the electronic road pricing system in 1998 – is now building the next-generation, satellite-based electronic road pricing system to be ready by 2020.

9   LTA is the public agency responsible for Singapore's land transport infrastructure and systems.

10   http://ezlink.com.sg.

11   www.pdpc.gov.sg/organisations/data-protection-officers.

12   Besides the ez-link card, the other stored-value card widely used in Singapore is issued by NETS. Also see "EZ-Link and NETS E-Payment: Creating a Standard and Building a Platform Innovation" by Christina Soh and Yvonne Chong, *Harvard Business Review*, 2013.

13   "Singapore Empowers Land Transport Planners with Data Warehouse," by Eric Thoo, Gartner Research, 18 October 2011.

14   Other than ez-link cards used by adult commuters, commuters may use other stored-value cards (such as NETS FlashPay) or concession cards (for children and senior citizens) that are not managed by EZ-Link.

15   See http://statutes.agc.gov.sg for more details on Singapore's Official Secrets Act (Chapter 213).

16   For example, the HIPAA Privacy Rule (45 CFR 164.514) from the US Department of Health and Human Services listed 18 data elements (also known as the HIPAA Safe Harbor data elements) that are direct identifiers that must be removed or generalised in a health record data set in order for it to be considered de-identified.

17   M. González, C. Hidalgo, & A.-L. Barabási, "Understanding Individual Human Mobility Patterns," *Nature*, 2008, 453:779–782.

18   Y.-A. de Montjoye et al., "Unique in the Crowd: The Privacy Bounds of Human Mobility," *Nature Scientific Reports*, 2013, 3:1376.

19   D. Barth-Jones, "The 'Re-Identification' of Governor William Weld's Medical Information: A Critical Re-Examination of Health Data Identification Risks and Privacy Protections, Then and Now," *SSRN Electronic Journal*, 2012.

20   A. Narayanan, "Robust De-Anonymization of Large Sparse Datasets." In: *Proceedings of the IEEE Symposium on Security and Privacy*, 2008.

21   C. Porter, "De-Identified Data and Third Party Data Mining: The Risk of Re-Identification of Personal Information," *Washington Journal of Law, Technology & Arts*, 2008, 5.

22   V. Pandurangan, "On Taxis and Rainbows – Lessons from NYC's improperly anonymized taxi logs", 22 June 2014, https://medium.com/@vijayp/of-taxis-and-rainbows-f6bc289679a1.

23   L. Sweeney, "*k*-Anonymity: A Model for Protecting Privacy," *International Journal on Uncertainty, Fuzziness and Knowledge-Based Systems*, 2002, 10:557–570.

24 C. Aggarwal, "On *k*-Anonymity and the Curse of Dimensionality." In: *Proceedings of the 31st International Conference on Very Large Databases (VLDB)*, 2005.

25 A. Machanavajjhala et al., "*l*-Diversity: Privacy beyond *k*-anonymity." In: *Proceedings of the 22nd International Conference on Data Engineering (ICDE)*, 2006.

26 N. Li, T. Li, & S. Venkatasubramanian, "*t*-Closeness: Privacy beyond *k*-Anonymity and *l*-Diversity." In: *Proceedings of the 23rd International Conference on Data Engineering (ICDE)*, 2007.

4 The analysis of data

From raw data to data products: a workflow

Figure 4.1 depicts the data analysis workflow of the case study in urban mobility. It is divided into two key phases: *data preparation*, followed by *data analytics*.

- *Data preparation phase.* The process of obtaining the raw data from the parties involved was discussed at length in the previous chapter. This is followed by detailed discussions with the data owners to develop an in-depth understanding of the meanings and definitions of the data fields in the data set, before proceeding to clean the data and integrate the data sets. Cleaning and integrating can be an iterative process – for example, data may need to be re-cleaned because of inconsistencies arising from integration with other data. When completed, the processed, cleaned, and aligned raw data is uploaded to an integrated data repository that supports efficient and scalable data storage and retrieval for the data analytics phase.
- *Data analytics phase.* The data is then explored to formulate hypotheses that may generate useful insights. This is supported by literature search, brainstorming, or by approaching the users for advice on the various possible classes of insights that they might wish to mine from the data. Computational models using statistical modelling and data-mining algorithms for interrogating the data are then designed and tested. The resulting insights are communicated to the users, who are the data owners as well, by generating informative visualisations and reports. Again, this is an iterative process. The outcomes of this phase are the "data products" that can be delivered to the data users. The data products can be in the form of visualisations and reports, or analytics software that the users can continue to use to generate visualisations and reports based on new data that may become available subsequently.

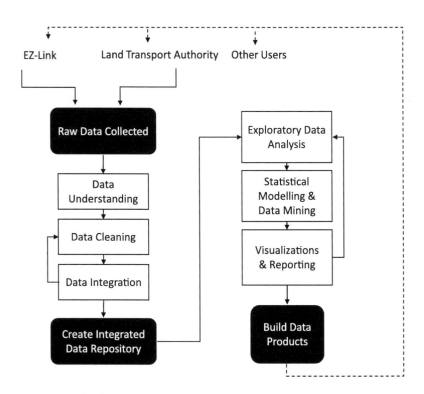

Figure 4.1 The data analytics process

The above data analysis workflow formed the structure of the tasks done on the smart card data obtained from EZ-Link and LTA. The data preparation phase requires the following:

- *Data understanding.* Data schema descriptions were obtained from the two data owners to understand the database structures, as well as the semantics of each of the data fields in the data sets. Sometimes, the data values in a data field had a complex structure that required further clarification. For example, in the EZ-Link data set, a data field named somewhat insignificantly as "BLOB_ID" actually contained key details about the MRT and LRT rides. However, it required a code translation table from the data owner for it to be deciphered. For example, the somewhat cryptic value "SMRT___00202082016004591" encodes an MRT trip with a tap out at station 002 (which further maps to the "Ang Mo Kio" MRT station) on 02 August 2016.

- *Data cleaning.* Next, data quality issues such as missing values, out-of-range values, duplicate entries, and so on were addressed by applying data-cleaning and quality-checking algorithms[1,2] to ensure that the data cleaning processes did not introduce new errors.
- *Data integration.* Both LTA and EZ-Link pre-anonymised their data sets independently. This meant that there were no common identifiers to join the two data sets directly. As described in the previous chapter, a matching algorithm was devised based on passengers' *tap-out location signatures.* In other words, the sequence of tap-out locations of an anonymous passenger's commute data was used to identify the same passenger in the other anonymised data set.

After the two data sets were properly cleaned and integrated, an Oracle[3] database for the integrated data set was designed and created. Database scripts for data import and extraction were created together with an index for rapid data retrieval. This led to the data analytics phase, which involved the following:

- *Exploratory data analysis.* Through a series of brainstorming exercises, a list of questions to interrogate the data was developed. In particular, the focus was on the possible descriptive statistics that could be derived from the data sets and would be useful to businesses, as well as predictive models that could be constructed from the given data. The literature on related work was also reviewed for specific directions and insights.
- *Statistical modelling and data mining.* Customised machine-learning and data-mining algorithms were then designed and implemented to extract the insights sought from the data set. The R scripting language was used for the complex data analysis.[4]
- *Visualisations and reporting.* During the data analytics phase, workshops were held with the stakeholders to share the visualisations and findings and to gather feedback that could be useful for further exploratory data analysis and for developing the final data products.

At the end of the data analytics phase, a software developer built data products based on the resulting transportation data analytics and the visualisation explored in the study. The data products have been implemented on a multi-user data exchange platform called A*DAX.[5] To efficiently deliver the data products to stakeholders and other users, these visualisations were implemented on a cloud platform – Amazon Web Services – so that they could be accessed by registered users through the Internet. Figure 4.2 shows the various analytics data products generated by the A*DAX system.

Barcharts: Taps Out on MRT

Dataset: MRTTapOuts

The total number of taps out at all MRT stations from January to March, 2016

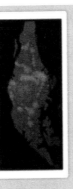

Stacked Barcharts: Passenger Types on MRT

Dataset: HeatmapMRTCommuterTypes

Three types of passengers: Students/Children, Senior Citizens and Torists at all MRT stations on March, 2016

Heat Map: Passenger Types on MRT

Dataset: HeatmapMRTCommuterTypes

Three types of passengers: Students/Children, Senior Citizens and Torists at all MRT stations on March, 2016

Waterfall Model: MRT Trips on Regions

Dataset: OD_MRT

MRT trips from one region to other regions of Singapore on March, 2016

Waterfall Model: Bus Trips on Regions

Dataset: OD_Bus

Bus trips from one region to other regions of Singapore on March, 2016

Pie Charts: Statistics for Singapore Public Transport

Dataset:

Statistics on public transport data of Singapore

TOP 5 TAP-OUTS (MRT/LRT)
OVERALL

Figure 4.2 Visualisation of data analytics outcomes

Source: Authors

Example analysis

Like most real-world data, the smart card data obtained from EZ-Link and LTA is a rich data set that has multiple facets for analysis. For example, it could be split into categories of the overall public transport spend. An interesting observation, as shown in Figure 4.3, is that the bus system has over half the total public transport spend. This means that despite the major developments in the rail networks in recent decades, the bus system still plays a key role for public transport commuters in Singapore. This is useful for transport planners, and one could then conduct deeper analysis of the fine-grained smart card data to uncover detailed commuter travel behaviours in order to better understand this phenomenon.

Smart card data could also be analysed through the lens of specific points of interest (POIs). The number of tap outs can be used as a proxy for foot traffic that arrived via public transportation at the POIs. Figure 4.4 shows a screen capture of the system's visualisation of the tap outs at various MRT stations and at different times.

When considering the three POIs of Orchard, Bugis, and Jurong (each represented by their respective MRT stations),[6] several features are observed. All three POIs are shopping destinations in Singapore, with Orchard being mostly for premier shopping, Bugis being mostly for local high street

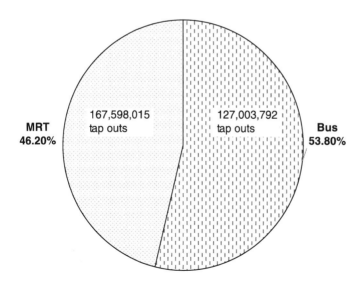

Figure 4.3 Public transit spend (January–March 2016)

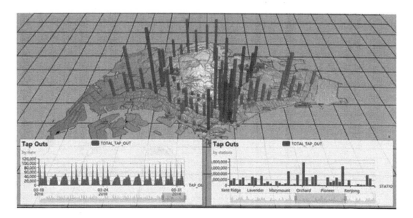

Figure 4.4 Tap outs at MRT stations at different times
Source: Authors

shopping, and Jurong being a suburban shopping destination. Orchard has a rich collection of shopping malls and hotels, Bugis has a mix of shopping malls and offices, and Jurong has offices and residential areas. The data for foot traffic that arrived at these three POIs via MRT was analysed on three different day categories: weekend, public holiday, and weekday.[7] The results are shown in Figure 4.5.

Not surprisingly, Orchard station emerges as the busiest weekend node of the three. This is as expected since Orchard is the grand dame of shopping destinations for both locals and tourists alike. On the other hand, it is interesting to note that for the public holiday, Bugis actually attracted more shoppers who arrived via MRT than Orchard. This surprising feature calls for a more detailed assessment of the reasons for such a difference. It could be due to factors such as a public holiday falling on Chinese New Year when most retail outlets in Orchard Road would be closed, but then that would also be the case in Bugis. So it could be that Bugis, on that day, attracted those who were not necessarily shoppers as much as those deciding to partake in hospitality and dining in the several local restaurants and other outlets in the city area. Such insights can be useful to both city planners as well as commercial businesses in those areas.

This insight can indeed be further enriched by overlaying the station-specific tap-out data with additional information such as demographic information[8] (Figure 4.6), as well as dwell time and other useful information that can be mined from the data. Businesses at the POIs can then use them to

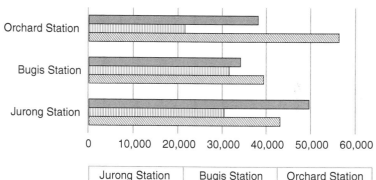

	Jurong Station	Bugis Station	Orchard Station
▦ Weekday	49,686	34,211	38,167
▥ Public holiday	30,457	31,596	21,583
▨ Weekend	43,170	39,456	56,386

▦ Weekday   ▥ Public holiday   ▨ Weekend

Figure 4.5 Visitors at selected POIs on registered cards

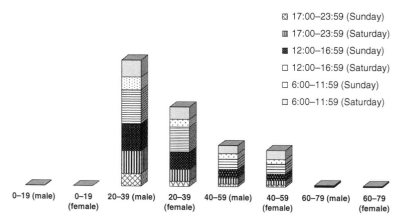

Figure 4.6 Foot traffic at Bugis: distribution by gender and age

derive detailed and localised strategies to better target specific customers at the right time and place.

A population or market segment-specific analysis on the data was also done. *Senior citizens* and *students* could be identified as segments from the data based on the concession travel cards that were given to these two specific groups of local travellers. As the tourism industry is a key economic driver for Singapore,[9] the *tourists* segment was also analysed. However, there was no special tourist card type in the data sets. Fortunately, as long as there are unique travel signatures for the travellers in a particular segment, it is possible to devise machine-learning algorithms to infer the market segment of interest. *Tourists* is one such market segment, as tourists travel to specific destinations such as tourist attractions much more frequently than the locals. A previously published algorithm[10] was implemented, and it used machine-learning techniques to iteratively filter out the inferred tourists from the local commuters in the data set.

Figure 4.7 shows the trip distributions for *senior citizens*, *students*, and *tourists* in the early morning (7:30 a.m.) of a weekday (Wednesday 9 March 2016). As expected, the destinations of the senior citizens were different from the students, while there were very minimal movements from the tourists early in the morning.

In contrast, the trip distributions for *senior citizens*, *students*, and *tourists* in the early evening (6:00 p.m.) of a day during the weekend (Sunday 13 March 2016) showed a different pattern, as shown in Figure 4.8. Unlike in the weekday mornings, both the *senior citizens* and the *students* actually shared relatively similar trip distributions in the evening, while the *tourists* were heading to different destinations from the locals. It was likely that the locals were wrapping up their weekend activities and going home, while for the tourists, the night was still young.

The above examples show that detailed insights about the population's travel behaviour can be extracted from the data set computationally using data mining, machine-learning algorithms, and visualisation. These insights are useful not only to the stakeholders in the transportation sector, but also to other stakeholders of the city, such as businesses, with the potential to generate new business opportunities.

In fact, there are already real-world use cases of business and social innovations using similar data sets. In Singapore, an experimental demand-driven transportation service called Beeline, which can be thought of as an "Uber for mini-buses," was developed based on analysis of the EZ-Link data to seed the initial bus routes.[11] A similar study of the night bus network was done in Seoul[12] where the mobile phone records of night travellers were used to identify key routes, design new lines, and optimise traffic intensity for a better pricing strategy. The new pricing regime benefited low-income groups while also reducing the need for car trips and improving the safety of women travellers. These examples show that the benefits of data analytics are not purely commercial, but also of a social value.

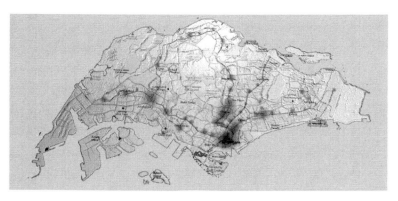

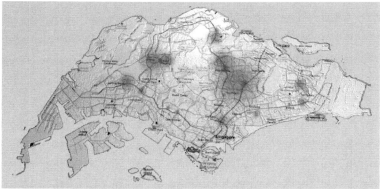

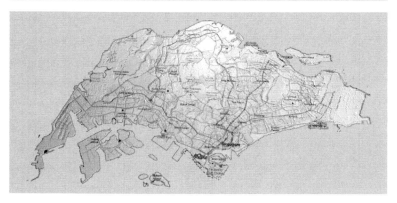

Figure 4.7 Trip distributions of *senior citizens* (top), *students* (middle), and
tourists (bottom) in the early morning (7:30 a.m.) of a weekday
(Wednesday 9 March 2016)

Source: Authors

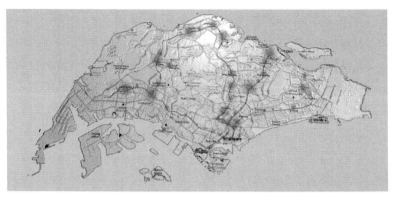

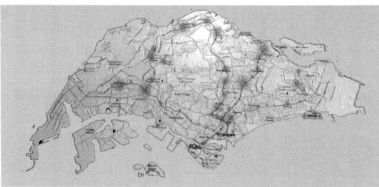

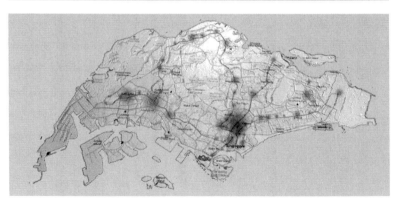

Figure 4.8 Trip distributions of *senior citizens* (top), *students* (middle), and *tourists* (bottom) in the early evening (6:00 p.m.) of a day during the weekend (Sunday 13 March 2016)

Source: Authors

Looking ahead: potential hurdles

In the journey towards a data economy, it is important to discover early the potential social, legal, and technological hurdles that may be encountered along the way. Three important potential issues need to be considered:

- *Data privacy and security.* Despite the liberal sharing of information on the Internet, privacy has remained a much-treasured fundamental right that is jealously protected by data protection laws. The increasing number of high-profile cases of data breaches highlights the shortcomings in data security. Yet, the data economy can only be realised through interactions with and transactions of data. There is a need to balance security and compliance risks for business with the need to use and even share data to formulate viable solutions and generate new economic opportunities, and at the same time, more sophisticated research efforts in data privacy and security will be required.
- *Data monopolies and accessibility.* The value of data or data products often increases with the size of the data. This preference for size has resulted in the rise of data titans such as Google and Facebook, which have captured major market shares of the data in their domains and developed high barriers to entry. Furthermore, data is often produced and collected in proprietary platforms and systems and is therefore not easily accessible. As data becomes a much sought-after commodity, there is a need to develop policies and technologies to support the democratisation[13] of data and to enable easy access to it, and this will be especially so if a vibrant data economy is to exist.
- *Algorithmic fairness and awareness.* The rise of the data economy and the advent of AI will lead to more algorithms being developed using data and deployed to mediate social processes, business transactions, governmental decisions, and so on. Many of these algorithms are "black boxes" that are empowered to make decisions without explanations, and there is often no transparency on the appropriateness of the data used to train these algorithms. This could lead to misplaced trust – computers, instructed by algorithms designed by humans and trained with data curated by humans, can still be fallible. As algorithms become an integral part of our lives, there is a need to develop policies and technologies to ensure algorithmic fairness and accountability. Importantly, there is a need to promote general data literacy so that people fully understand how their data is being collected and used for both commercial and social purposes.

Emerging technologies

Technology is clearly at the centre stage of the data economy. The advances in technologies such as the Internet and the, cloud, mobile, and big data computing, data analytics, machine learning, and AI have played key roles in powering the rise of the data economy.

Technology and the scientific community that develops it will continue to play definitive roles in addressing the issues and challenges that will be encountered in the journey towards a viable data economy. Some of the promising emerging technologies that could be useful in addressing issues that were highlighted earlier are given below.

Differential privacy

In the previous chapter, concerns regarding current approaches to privacy preservation such as de-identification were raised. It was noted that they have failed to provide adequate privacy protection. Researchers have since embarked on the development of foundational approaches to private data analysis, and one promising approach emerging from the privacy research community is *differential privacy*.

Differential privacy[14] provides a rigorous mathematical treatment of privacy that makes it possible to provide strong theoretical guarantees on both the privacy and utility of data sets that are released with differential privacy data treatment techniques. The techniques typically involve statistical noise-generating mechanisms that can be applied to a data set with the assurance that a statistical query to the data set will produce a given result with nearly the same probability regardless of whether it is conducted on a data set with an individual's information or not. In other words, the differential privacy framework provides mathematically provable assurance that the risk to one's privacy will not be substantially increased as a result of one's participation in a statistical database. In this way, data scientists can mine useful and sufficiently accurate statistical insights from the mathematically treated data sets while providing strong, mathematically proven assurance to the data contributors that the risk of privacy loss is minimised.

While the concept of differential privacy has received considerable attention in the research community, there have not been many mainstream differential privacy applications due to the complexity of its underlying mathematical concepts. It has only recently started to come out of the confines of theoretical settings – for example, Apple has announced[15] the use of differential privacy to help discover the usage patterns from a large number of users without compromising individual privacy.

There is often a long journey from theory to practice for the researchers taking the less-travelled path of rigorous foundational approaches. However, for solving the hard and complex problems such as data privacy, deep fundamental scientific research is essential, and investments in such research are necessary for building a robust data economy.

Secure multi-party computation

In supporting the democratisation of data, data platforms should provide secure sharing of data such that collective data aggregation and analysis becomes possible even in the light of legal and corporate restrictions on data sharing.

A promising technology for addressing the above is *secure multi-party computation* or SMC. In a multi-party computation, there are multiple (say n) data owners p_1, p_2, ..., p_n, wanting to jointly compute the value of a publicly shared function F[16] on their private data sets d_1, d_2,..., d_n. SMC techniques allow $F(d_1, d_2,..., d_n)$ to be derived while allowing the data owners to keep their inputs securely secret.

Unlike differential privacy, SMC is not an emerging technology – the theoretical constructs for it were first proposed more than 30 years ago,[17] and since then there has been active research in this area, especially by the cryptography research community, with much focus on security. However, just like differential privacy, SMC has strong theoretical foundations, but the gaps for translating theory into practice can be quite daunting. For mainstream adoption of the technologies, there are many practical issues that need to be taken into consideration. For example, in practice, the system performance, especially on big data, becomes a key consideration that is as important as security. As multi-party computation uses cryptographic techniques heavily, the computation time to encrypt big data can be a major bottleneck. Many of the proposed multi-party computation frameworks only allow online computations; in other words, each involved party must be available during the secure computation. This may not be feasible in practice. Furthermore, techniques are often designed to serve specific purposes and are difficult to reuse, making it difficult to achieve widespread adoption.

SMC can be a promising technology for confidential data collection and analysis. Recently, the Estonian Tax and Customs Board built a tax fraud detection system prototype that uses SMC to remove companies' concerns over the confidentiality of their purchase and sales invoice data.[18] In Boston, a web-based application using SMC was deployed to support the aggregation of sensitive salary data in order to identify possible salary inequities.[19] By taking a user-centric approach,[20] complex technologies like multi-party computation can be effectively deployed to create real-world impacts.

In recent years, SMC has also caught the attention of research communities beyond the cryptography community. The database community has begun to develop databases that support multi-party computation with a focus on scalability and efficiency. Such cross-disciplinary research that combines the works of security research and database research are important to developing systems in practice. A recently published work proposes the Private Data Network,[21] which is a federated database for querying the collective data of mutually distrustful parties. The system combines database technologies with SMC by translating SQL[22] statements into SMC primitives to compute the desired query results over all the source databases without revealing sensitive information about individual data records to each other. In addition, the recent popularity and acceptance of blockchain technologies also provides great promise for moving SMC from the realm of theory to practice.[23]

Adversarial machine learning

Data is the raw material for the data economy, and machine learning is the technological engine that turns the raw data into useful insights and predictions. Machine learning gives the computer the ability to automatically learn from example data generated previously for a particular task and to build analytical models for decision support or for extracting insights from similar data in the future.

Researchers have continued to unleash the power of machine learning – recently, advanced machine learning (e.g. deep learning) has enabled machines to achieve human-level performance and beyond.[24] While researchers continue to expand the boundaries of what technologies can achieve and incorporate them into our daily lives, it is equally important to understand the perils that a dependency on the technologies may bring with their widespread adoption.

Just like human beings, technologies have their own shortcomings and weaknesses. For instance, it has been shown by researchers that machine learning can be gamed in more than one way. By understanding how computer programs recognise objects, the knowledge gained can be exploited to trick the computers into seeing things that are obviously not there,[25] or misrecognising a person as someone completely different.[26] Search engines can also be manipulated through techniques such as "Google bombing" and "spamdexing." A recent report co-authored by 26 experts from a wide range of disciplines and organisations spanning academia, civil society, and industry warns of the potential malicious uses of AI and of the urgency of addressing this issue.[27]

The emerging field of adversarial machine learning aims to address the so-called "AI security" or "AI safety" issues by exploring and exposing the vulnerabilities of using machine-learning techniques. For example, using adversarial machine learning, researchers have demonstrated that images that are protected using standard obfuscation techniques such as mosaicking and blurring to make them unrecognisable by human eyes can actually be re-identified by computer programs using deep learning.[28] With the broad adoption of machine learning, more research into adversarial machine learning needs to be done to expose, understand, and hopefully mitigate the vulnerabilities of machine-learning algorithms and applications.

Algorithmic fairness and explainability

In a data economy, data and algorithms based on data will be used not just for generating economic value for business, but also for policy-making and developing social programmes. In addition to privacy preservation, it is important to ensure that the computerised algorithms are aligned with our other social and moral value systems, including ethical issues such as fairness.

While the computer may appear impartial given that it only computes mathematically and algorithmically, the algorithms are created by human designers. Even if the algorithms are generated based entirely on the data that is given, the curation of the data is still done by humans. There could be intentional bias in the design of the computerised algorithms or the curation of the data due to human designers' particular value systems. There could also be inherent historical biases and societal priorities that are unwittingly embedded into the data that is fed into a computer. This is so with big data, which may already show a specific bias in the way it has been collected and curated. Such biases could result in the computerised algorithms recommending or even executing choices under the veils of mathematical algorithms, which are often presented as "black boxes" to the common folks, reinforcing possibly harmful and unfair implicit biases. For example, it is possible that a job recommendation program trained on big data may further recommend more high-paying job opportunities to a particular gender or ethnic groups due to some current bias in the underlying data.

As such, researchers developing the technologies for the data economy have to not only focus on the performance of their algorithms, but also investigate and reveal the potential impacts of algorithmic bias and move beyond the "black box" approach towards better algorithmic explainability, interpretability, and transparency. There are some initial efforts in this direction. The Association for Computing Machinery (ACM) US Public Policy Council and ACM Europe Policy Committee have recently issued a joint statement highlighting the potential harm of algorithmic bias, as well as a list of seven principles to foster algorithmic transparency and accountability.[29] Researchers have also started to study ways to mathematically quantify ethical concepts such as fairness[30] and to design machine-learning methods[31] that ensure equality of opportunity. The students of the first AI undergraduate degree in the United States, offered by Carnegie Mellon University where AI was invented, will also study the ethical and societal implications of AI in addition to the technical aspects.

Beyond technologies

In the data economy, businesses can afford to provide their services at a very low cost (or even for free) because the data generated through their business activities is often much more valuable than the business services themselves. As end users, the free and individualised services are simply too enticing and oftentimes are addictive. It is only recently that we have begun to get a few good glimpses of the darker sides of the data-driven world (e.g. the Cambridge Analytica saga). In the era of big data, in order for the data economy to be viable, businesses in the data economy must realise their moral responsibility and educate the end users on the implications of "data asymmetries" where the computers (and the businesses behind them) learn a lot about us, and yet the majority of us know very little about these algorithms and the data that the computer used to learn about us, as well as how the data may be repurposed for other uses that we may not be aware of.

The arrival of a data economy will certainly lead to technology being at the centre stage of many economic, social, cultural, and political activities. The technologists, who are the human designers of the algorithms, have to become socially responsible and be mindful of the ramifications of these technologies, not only in terms of scientific advancements, but also in terms of the associated social, economic, and legal concerns. At the same time, the policy-makers and the other stakeholders of the data economy (including businesses and citizens) must be empowered with a confident understanding of what technologies can and cannot do, and with a clear awareness of the possible new perils that such technologies may bring.

For example, in devising the privacy laws for the data economy, policy-makers should be aware of how emerging technologies such as differential privacy and SMC may address some of these issues, as well as the possibility of other new issues arising, such as adversarial machine learning and algorithmic bias, which have been described earlier. As data and technologies become integral parts of our lives, technologies must evolve from being "black boxes" understood by few and be made accessible to a broad audience both conceptually and technologically. This is essential for developing a viable data economy.

Three issues have been highlighted as potential hurdles in the trajectory towards a viable data economy. These issues centre on the need for balancing transparency and privacy with the aim of ensuring a seamless world of economic and social transactions. This is not an easy proposition simply because the trade-offs are not clear, and there is an asymmetry in the information available to individuals at any given time. All the more so, then, that a level playing field must be created to prevent misuses of data and its valuable insights. The next chapter builds on these issues and looks at some of the defining features of the legal contours that inform the boundaries of the data economy.

Notes

1 C.M. Teng, "Combining Noise Correction with Feature Selection." In: *International Conference on Data Warehousing and Knowledge Discovery*, 2003, 340–349
2 T.M. Khoshgoftaar & P. Rebours, "Improving Software Quality Prediction by Noise Filtering Techniques," *Journal of Computer Science and Technology*, 2007, 22:387–396
3 Commercial database management system that can handle big data in terms of data loading, acquisition, management, storage, integration, presentation, and analysis.
4 R is a popular data analytics tool that supports many statistical (e.g. classical statistical tests and non-linear and linear regression) and data mining (e.g. classification, clustering, time-series analysis, and graphical models) techniques to analyse big data. It also integrates with Oracle easily.
5 W.S. Ng, P.M.C. Lim, S.-K. Ng, H. Wu, & S. Xiang, "A*DAX for Transport Data Management, Sharing and Analytics." Presented at: *21st ITS World Congress*, Detroit, IL, USA, 7–11 September 2014.
6 For Jurong, the station selected is Jurong East MRT station.
7 The actual dates are: 19 January 2016 (weekday – Tuesday), 23 January 2016 (weekend – Saturday), and 8 February 2016 (public holiday – Chinese New Year).
8 EZ-Link's registered user information has been used here for demonstration.
9 Singapore's tourism receipts were S$24.8 billion in 2016 (*The Straits Times*, February 14, 2017).
10 M. Xue, H. Wu, W. Chen, W.S. Ng, & G.H. Goh, "Identifying Tourists from Public Transport Commuters." In: *Proceedings of the 20th ACM SIGKDD International Conference on Knowledge Discovery and Data Mining*, 2014.

11   www.imda.gov.sg/infocomm-and-media-news/buzz-central/2016/6/ smart-nation-big-on-big-data.

12   http://dataimpacts.org.

13   Data democratisation means breaking down silos and providing access to data when and where it is needed at any given moment (Beginner's Guide to Data Democratization, channels.theinnovationenterprise.com).

14   C. Dwork, "A Firm Foundation for Private Data Analysis," *Communications of the ACM*, 2011, 54:86–95.

15   J. Evans, "What Apple Users Need to Know about Differential Privacy." In: *Computerworld*, 27 June 2016.

16   For example, F could be average, min, or max.

17   D. Chaum, C Crépeau, & I. Damgård, "Multiparty Unconditionally Secure Protocols." In: *Proceedings of the 20th ACM symposium on Theory of computing (STOC)*, 1988.

18   D. Bogdanov et al., "How the Estonian Tax and Customs Board Evaluated a Tax Fraud Detection System Based on Secure Multi-Party Computation." In: *Proceedings of the International Conference on Financial Cryptography and Data Security*, 2015.

19   R. Barlow, "Computational Thinking Breaks a Logjam – Hariri Institute Helps Address Boston's Male–Female Pay Gap." In: *BU Today*, 27 April 2015.

20   A. Bestavros, A. Lapets, & M. Varia, "User-Centric Distributed Solutions for Privacy-Preserving Analytics," *Communications of the ACM*, 2017, 60: 37–39.

21   J. Bater et al., "SMCQL: Secure Querying for Federated Databases," *Proceedings of the VLDB Endowment*, 2017, 10:673–684.

22   SQL stands for Structured Query Language. It is a standard computer language for communicating with relational database management systems.

23   G. Zyskind, "Efficient Secure Computation Enabled by Blockchain Technology," PhD dissertation report, Massachusetts Institute of Technology, 2016.

24   For example, AI software programs built with machine-learning algorithms have been shown to defeat the top human players in a wide array of complex games from chess (1996) to Jeopardy (2011), Go (2016), and Poker (2017).

25   A. Nguyen, J. Yosinski, & J. Clune, "Deep Neural Networks Are Easily Fooled: High Confidence Predictions for Unrecognizable Images." In: *Computer Vision and Pattern Recognition (CVPR)*, 2015.

26   M. Sharif, S. Bhagavatula, L. Bauer, & M. Reiter, "Accessorize to a Crime: Real and Stealthy Attacks on State-of-the-Art Face Recognition." In: *Proceedings of the 23rd ACM Conference on Computer and Communications Security (CCS)*, 2016.

27   M. Brudage et al., "The Malicious Use of Artificial Intelligence: Forecasting, Prevention, and Mitigation," 2018.

28   R. McPherson, R. Shokri, & V. Shmatikov, "Defeating Image Obfuscation with Deep Learning." In: arXiv:1609.0040, 2016.

29   Statement on Algorithmic Transparency and Accountability by ACM U.S. Public Policy Council, approved 12 January 2017, and ACM Europe Policy

Committee, approved 25 May 2017. www.acm.org/binaries/content/assets/public-policy/2017_joint_statement_algorithms.pdf.

30 C. Dwork et al., "Fairness through Awareness." In: *Proceedings of the 3rd Innovations in Theoretical Computer Science Conference (ITCS)*, 2012.

31 M. Hardt, E. Price, & N. Srebo, "Equality of Opportunity in Supervised Learning." In: arXiv:1610.02413, 2016.

5 The legal contours of the data economy

There has been increasing interest in the legal protection offered to individuals and private entities when data becomes an integral feature of transactions, economic or otherwise, between and among participants in the data economy. There are important privacy trade-offs when personal data is aggregated and analysed together with the data of other consumers.[1] This also raises issues on whether individuals are willingly providing their personal data or are being pressured to do so on the premise that other services will be made available to them if they do so or that the services they want will not otherwise be forthcoming. The legal structure of privacy protection attempts to provide some guidance on how these features should be perceived and how the attendant trade-offs should be addressed. This chapter draws on the various privacy issues that have arisen in the case study, with a focus largely on Singapore.

The current legal regime that defines data collection, usage, and sharing (collectively referred to as data management or data handling)

Singapore enacted its first and only wide-ranging and comprehensive baseline data protection law and regulations in 2012 after about a decade of study into the impacts and implications of such a regime on the collection, use, and sharing of such data on the economy.

The Personal Data Protection Act (Act 26 of 2012) (PDPA) entered into force in stages, with the administrative structure put in place first, followed by the Do Not Call (DNC) provisions and finally the Data Protection (DP) regime in 2014. This was to provide a reasonable period for the organisations that would have to comply with the PDPA to understand the Act and put into place measures to comply with its requirements. In the meantime, the Personal Data Protection Commission (PDPC) was also set up to provide advisory guidelines to provide further elucidation of the law.

This was important as it will be some time before the courts get involved in interpreting the provisions of the Act to provide more clarity on the standards and parameters of protection, which are currently ambiguous, to an extent.

Even though international instruments and institutions such as the OECD and Asia-Pacific Economic Cooperation (APEC) provide for general concepts and principles for data protection, it is left to national (and, in the case of the EU, regional) lawmakers to define and set the standards of protection and to define the entities that have to observe the restrictions, as well as the extent of the obligation. The core values of consent, control, and care, which are primarily defined by the concepts of consent, notification, and purpose, and are covered by the various core obligations as defined by legislation, are by and large common to all data protection laws. However, the actual scope of protection varies across jurisdictions. Where there are similarities in socioeconomic and cultural policies, similar concepts in other jurisdictions, particularly in Asia, can be helpful. This is especially so when the data protection and DNC regimes are defined mainly by two considerations: the sociocultural background of the country and region concerned on the one hand and the pressures of global harmonisation and standards on the other. There may be tensions between the two considerations. The sociocultural background of Asian nations, in particular those with similar economies and interests, especially Hong Kong, Taiwan, South Korea, and Japan, are thus particularly relevant to defining the DP landscape in the region and for Singapore in time to come.

The Singapore PDPA provides for the protection of "personal data." "Personal data" is defined as "data, whether true or not, about an individual who can be identified from that data; or from that data and other information to which the organisation has or is likely to have access."[2] The obligations under the PDPA can be avoided either by not identifying a set of data as personal in nature or by excluding the subject from the application of the Act. The latter is more straightforward, as the organisations or individuals are excluded by categories under Section 4 of the Act in a manner that is quite clear in most instances and, if not, is made clear in subsidiary legislation, as is the case for "public agencies,"[3] and through enforcement decisions by the Commissioner. The former is more ambiguous as the definition of personal data is open to interpretation. This is where this study has been most careful when it comes to the use of data provided by its sources, both public and private. In some cases, data "about" or "relating to" an individual is read conjunctively with the identifiability of an individual from that data, but in others it can be read as separate or disjunctive elements. The ability to read those requirements in a strict and narrow manner, or in a flexible and purposive manner, adds complexity to the issue. Moreover, even when information falls under the scope of "personal data," there may not be a violation of PDPA obligations if the standards set in relation to each of the obligations are met.[4] The common test found in the Act is the "reasonableness test." Generally, to comply with the Act and "in meeting its responsibilities under this Act, an organisation shall consider what a reasonable person would consider appropriate in the circumstances."[5] Thus, for example, "[a]n organisation may collect, use or disclose personal data about an individual only for purposes that a reasonable person would consider appropriate in the circumstances,"[6] and only if that the individual has been notified or informed in accordance with the notification obligation.[7]

It should be noted that there are also partial exemptions (mainly from the consent requirement) from each obligation – including and in particular the collection, use, and disclosure obligations – under the Act, which, if eligible, can be used to reduce one's obligations under the Act.[8] There is also a deemed consent provision that allows organisations managing and handling personal data to extend consent "artificially" to situations where it is "reasonable that the individual would voluntarily provide the data" for a purpose when there is no actual consent. This is another example of the compromise that the Act makes in weighing the interests of individuals and organisations, particularly businesses.

The purpose of the PDPA is explicitly stated in the Act as one that is "to govern the collection use and disclosure of personal data by organisations in a manner that recognises both the right of individuals to protect their personal data and the need of organisations to collect, use or disclose personal data for purposes that a reasonable person would consider appropriate in the circumstances."[9] This is important as it forms the basis for any interpretation of the provisions of the Act. Although it appears to favour a balance-of-interests approach to the Act, there are cogent arguments for a broad and expansive approach to the concept of "personal data."[10] Be that as it may, the approach that has been taken to ensure compliance (under Section 4.2 of the PDPA) in the current study is the more stringent one in order to ensure that the data economy project does not fall foul of the law.[11]

It must also be noted that while the public agencies providing data for the purpose of the research in the study are not covered by the Act,[12] the PDPA nevertheless is relevant. First, the study team, as recipients of the information and those who will make further use of it, has to comply with the requirements of the PDPA; and second, the public agency, namely LTA, will have to observe similar standards of protection set by the government.[13] Needless to say, EZ-Link Pte Ltd has to comply with the law in relation to the release of any data for the study (either by legal compliance or avoidance of the PDPA obligations).

Another concept that is central to the PDPA is the concept of "reasonableness" (and "practicableness" or "appropriateness," where relevant), as it sets the standard of compliance and hence the threshold for liability.[14] This concept appears central to the compliance threshold for data protection in other jurisdictions such as Hong Kong. This provides leeway and flexibility for collection, use, and compliance where it may not be practicable or reasonable to expect organisations to obtain actual consent, given the circumstances of the case.

As shall be noted, a more generous interpretation of personal data (for organisations) is to exclude identifiable data on the basis of a lack of intended and actual focus on an individual, such as through individual characterisation or relevance to the study at hand.

Directly identifiable information such as name, identity card number, passport number, image, and biometric data are "personal data"; other information such as financial and health records are also peculiar to an individual. Secondary materials such as profiling information that pins down the unique characteristic of a particular individual such as his or her habits, location or travel data, and personal interests are also personal information whether by themselves or together with other information accessible to the organisation concerned. Contact information can also be identifiable information if it is not shared by more than one individual, and other legal obligations can also apply in this regard under the DNC regime and the Spam Control Act (Cap. 311A), the former in relation to voice calls and text messages and the latter in relation to electronic mail and text messages.

The challenges posed by data acquisition and analytics under the current PDPA of 2012 and the implications of private–public data interface

This study has taken a multi-pronged approach to compliance with the PDPA. Other studies that may involve the collection, use, and disclosure of data in a manner that is more diverse will require an adjustment to this approach.

First, this study takes the approach that the intentions and purpose of the use of the data in relation to the data analysis and goals of the study are not focused on personal data or on particular individuals, at least at this stage of this project. With reference to Singapore's definition of "personal data," if this is relevant to (and read into) the reasonableness obligation, it provides an alternative protection from the effects of the legislation. This is the Hong Kong approach in the *Newsweek* case.[15] Moreover, as this study was focused on aggregated data based on categories or groups (e.g. students, the elderly, tourists, and the usual adults segments) in its data analysis and results, there is no violation of personal privacy in the sense that the management and handling of such data would not be considered unreasonable or inappropriate by a Singaporean citizen or resident in the context of the study and circumstances of this case.

Second, in practice, the data sets and schema were anonymised by both agencies at their physical premises by their own officers before they were transferred for the study. That is, what could potentially constitute personal data was scrubbed of identifiable information at the premises and point of collection of the primary or source agency. In fact, the anonymisation process was done by, and within, EZ-Link and LTA. For proper control and handover, as noted, anonymisation was done on site by EZ-Link's own privacy officer and employee, and the data was reviewed by EZ-Link personnel before it was copied onto a CD-ROM and handed over for data analysis proper at the study laboratory. In relation to LTA data, LTA did not share their data schema as EZ-Link had done. Likewise, LTA anonymised and sanitised their data set before it was transferred to the team. As such, there were no sensitive data fields given for the study.

In relation to EZ-Link data, each data field (as well as each set of data) was identified separately as "potentially sensitive"; that is, as possibly constituting personal data for the purpose of the PDPA and for the purpose of anonymisation. An "appropriate" and as such "reasonable" and "practicable" anonymisation technique was provided for each of the identified sensitive data fields, but it was left to the primary agency to anonymise the data on site of the source (which does not constitute collection or use, but rather processing) before digitally transferring (or disclosing) the anonymised data to the team for their use in analysis. The final step is important as it provides an additional layer of protection by reducing the risk of re-identification through reverting the data to its original form. The study proposed the "*k*-anonymity" technique for generalisation or suppression of each sensitive data field (where appropriate and suitable), which is also arguably one that is reasonable (and practicable) within the context of the type of data concerned and the study of the data.[16]

Although it is possible for anyone to whom the data set is made available to use elaborate technical means to re-identify or reconstruct the anonymised data in relation to an individual, this cannot be done to the majority of the individuals; the information from sources cannot itself be reconstructed completely to identify individuals; expertise, technical know-how, and considerable effort is required to match the data sets with other information in order to do so (and hence this is not practicable or reasonable). "Publicly available" personal data, if used to re-identify individuals, is not personal data for the purposes of the PDPA in relation to the consent requirement for collection, use, and disclosure.[17] Finally, the data is arguably not sensitive enough to elicit complaints. Moreover, there is no intention to reverse the process in order to identify specific individuals. Hence, the risk of legal liability is extremely low.

In this study, a matching algorithm was developed to link the data sets from EZ-Link and LTA (CRD_NUM and CAN numbers, respectively) in order to analyse the data sets to produce the information in Chapters 3 and 4. The categories do not identify individuals and are not about individuals, but rather focus on groups and their locations and movements.

Third, there will not be any issue with the further disclosure and transfer of the outcomes of the research, as it does not contain personal data as its intended focus or in its results. However, it should be noted that in relation to further studies that deal with personal data or that have personally identifiable data as their focus, particularly if the goal of the data analysis is to provide inputs for marketing or outreach purposes (and in relation to which an individual's identity is required),[18] then both the DP and DNC regimes are applicable. In relation to this, as will be explained later in this chapter, in order for the law to facilitate, or at least not be an impediment to, the data economy in such exploitation of data, it will be necessary to either comply with its requirements or for the PDPA to institute additional and new exceptions to accommodate such uses and disclosures to third parties.

Finally, in the meantime (and more relevant to the current study), it should also be noted that there might be partial exemptions from consent even in the unlikely event that the collection, use, and disclosure of data falls under the purview of the PDPA. For example, the exceptions under the Second,[19] Third,[20] and Fourth[21] Schedules of the Act for personal data that are "necessary for evaluative purposes" (for collection, use, and disclosure) and that are "used for a research purpose, including historical or statistical research" (for use and disclosure) can relieve researchers of the consent obligation.[22] This is also noteworthy (as well as when considering the limits and conditions) if future studies do involve personal data handling by organisations that fall under the coverage of the PD regime.

The specific relationship between the current 2012 PDPA laws and regulations on the study and analysis of data from contactless smart cards

The focus of this book is specifically on the lessons learnt from the management of data relating to contactless smart cards, particularly from the mistakes made by the entities concerned that were involved in any point of the handling of the data, whether it was related to collection, use, sharing, disclosure, or other matters. These can provide guidelines on such data management as well as highlighting others in the event that the PDPA strengthens protections (e.g. by extending coverage to the public sector) and in relation to the sharing of more "sensitive information" (e.g. payment or financial information, which may have stronger protections under other laws or regulations). These measures may also guide the PDPC and lawmakers when deciding on changes to the regime, whether in terms of expanding protections and/or where additional general exceptions or partial exemptions (especially from the consent requirement for collection, use, or disclosure) should be made to facilitate the data economy objectives, taking into consideration a whole range of other interests (sometimes complementary, sometimes competing).

EZ-Link Pte Ltd

EZ-Link is an organisation for the purposes of the Singapore PDPA. As such, it has to comply with the requirements of the Act. EZ-Link thus has a practice of not collecting personal data from its clients and customers as much as is possible or practicable. Where it does, the collection is purpose-based (e.g. for insurance), and even then it is for purposes within its purview or control. For example, for automatic topping up purposes, it is EZ-Link's partner bank that collects personal data, including sensitive financial information, from users; likewise, for use of EZ-Link cards as access cards to buildings, the security provider partnered with EZ-Link collects and stores the user information.

Other information collected such as location data (tap-out information) and payment data (library fines, retail or vending machine payments) are linked to the card, but are not further traceable to the person holding the card. That is, the card is not linked to an individual normally (and can thus be "transferable" legitimately or otherwise), unless the user opts for the insurance option.

LTA (and Transit Link Pte Ltd)

LTA is a "public agency" and is exempt from the PDPA. The government has its own protocols for the protection of sensitive data, including personal data, and these protocols provide the reason and justification for the exemption. In all likelihood, the exclusion of public agencies also has much to do with logistics and the administrative burden of compliance. There is potential for its inclusion in the future.

Transit Link is a subsidiary of LTA and provides integrated services and solutions to all transport stakeholders including authorities like LTA, public transport operators, card managers including EZ-Link, and transport users.

Its operations include the processing of transport data relating to transit transactions, revenue apportionment (to public transport operators) and card transactions (e.g. sale, refund, and top-up of stored-value cards). The LTA collects data from various sources including the card readers used on buses and for MRT services.

Transit Link collects personal data through various ways, both physical and digital. The type of personally identifiable information collected and the notification of purpose for the collection, use, and disclosure of personal data is provided on their website. Use (and disclosure) generally relates to one or more of the following purposes[23]: the supply of services; identification and verification purposes in connection with any of the services that may be supplied; for the provision of online services; to provide users with access to specific information; and to contact users regarding their enquiries or feedback.

The lessons from and implications of the global data protection trend and standards on data acquisition and analytics for data economy projects

Two things should be noted at this point: first, the focus of the current study relates to the management of data within the Singapore jurisdiction. If the data subject or the data flow extends beyond Singapore, there may be implications for the compliance with the laws in other jurisdictions. Second, the local DP regime must meet minimal international data protection standards in order to ensure the smooth trans-border flow of data from other countries and for data analytics involving data collected or stored overseas to proceed unimpeded and without the threat of blockage of information flow from another jurisdiction that may have stronger and more protectionist measures in place for data protection for data subjects.

Hence, the study of both the parameters and standards of protection in other jurisdictions is also important in order to better understand differences in regimes as well as the global trends and standards that studies on the data economy should adhere to, both to meet local standards and to anticipate changes in requirements. The focus in this chapter will be on Asian jurisdictions that have a similar form of legislation and an almost similar sociocultural make-up to Singapore. These jurisdictions would also have a policy focus on the development of a smart nation that resembles Singapore's current efforts, and their use of contactless smart cards will also be considered. However, the EU's General Data Protection Regulation (GDPR), which was approved by the EU Parliament on 14 April 2016 and entered into effect on 25 May 2018, must also be referred to in relation to the above points given its implications for trans-border data flows and its wider impact on the future standards and expectations of data protection obligations.

Global trends and standards

Hong Kong

Hong Kong as a study of data protection (or, in the case of the territory, data privacy) is unique and integral to an Asian perspective as it was one of the earliest Asian jurisdictions to adopt comprehensive laws on this subject and also advanced protections, public education, and enforcement by the Privacy Commissioner. In Hong Kong, the overarching legal framework as it relates to data protection is provided by the Data Protection (Privacy) Ordinance (PDPO), which was enacted in 1995 by the British colonial administration prior to Hong Kong's handover to China in July 1997. The PDPO as it was enacted drew inspiration primarily from the OECD Privacy Guidelines and EU Directive on Data Protection. Although it was enacted in 1995, the PDPO only entered into force from 1997 and over three stages.

In terms of its substantive coverage, the PDPO comprises six Data Protection Principles that broadly reflect the OECD Privacy Guidelines. In this regard, these principles apply to both private and public entities and, unlike certain other jurisdictions such as the UK, include both automated and non-automated data or processing.

Specifically, these six principles are:

1. Collection Purpose and Means principle, which stipulates that personal data shall not be collected unless the collection is necessary and directly related to a lawful purpose directly related to a function or activity of the data user who is to use the data and not excessive in relation to that purpose;
2. Accuracy and Retention principle, which, inter alia, requires personal data to be accurate with regards to the purpose for which the personal data is or is to be used and that personal data shall not be kept longer than is necessary for the fulfilment of the purposes for which the data is or is to be used;
3. Use principle, which requires that the prescribed consent of the data subject be obtained before the data can be used for the fulfilment of the purpose for which collection was based on a purpose directly related to the foregoing;
4. Security principle, which requires all practicable steps be taken to ensure that personal data held by a data user is protected against unauthorised or accidental use;

5. Openness principle, which stipulates that all practicable steps be taken to ensure that a person can find out a data user's data protection policies and practices and be informed about the kind of personal data relating to such a person held by the data user and the main purposes for the retention and use of such personal data; and
6. Data Access and Correction principle, which obliges a person to be generally granted access to personal data held by a data user and for erroneous data held by a data user to be corrected.

As the name of the ordinance suggests, the PDPO contemplates the protection of individual privacy, but it is not clear what this translates to in concrete terms. The PDPO has hitherto not been used to provide a wider right of privacy protection, nor has it been amended to reflect in its principles a broader view of privacy as opposed to convention data protection. The trend from its implementation through cases and the work of the Hong Kong Privacy Commissioner for Personal Data (PCPD) suggest that they take a more pragmatic approach to the matter, particularly with the Special Administrative Region's Smart City initiative.[24]

Notwithstanding this, there are other recourses to the right of privacy under Hong Kong law. Most notably, this can be found under the Basic Law of Hong Kong, a legal instrument of Hong Kong of constitutional status. Specifically, the Basic Law provides that:

1. "The homes and other premises of Hong Kong residents shall be inviolable," and that "arbitrary or unlawful search of, or intrusion into [such homes and premises] shall be prohibited"[25]; and
2. "The freedom and privacy of communication of Hong Kong residents shall be protected by law," and that "No department or individual may … infringe upon the freedom and privacy of communications of residents except that the relevant authorities may inspect communication in accordance with legal procedures to meet the needs of public security or of investigation into criminal offences."[26]

In addition, the Basic Law is also important as it preserves Hong Kong's status as a common law jurisdiction and, in this way, allows for Hong Kong courts to look to other common law jurisdictions to provide greater protection to privacy, such as through the expansion of the law of the breach of confidence, a route that UK courts have taken. In the UK, courts expanded the common law to cover privacy by basing the confidentiality of information on whether there is a reasonable expectation of privacy as regards the information, therefore effectively creating a back door to a general tort of privacy.

Besides the Basic Law, persons may also seek limited protection under the Bill of Rights Ordinance, which was enacted in 1991, but this ordinance applied only to public authorities, not private entities.

The PDPO defines "personal data" broadly and does not have explicit territorial limitations, although there are practical limitations when it comes to investigations and enforcement through some link to the territory, such as the data subject or data user's links to Hong Kong. "Personal data" is defined under Section 2(1) of the PDPO to mean "any data – (a) relating directly or indirectly to a living individual; (b) from which it is practicable for the identity of the individual to be directly or indirectly ascertained; and (c) in a form in which access to or processing of the data is practicable."

As acknowledged by the Privacy Commissioner as the enforcement authority of the PDPO, whilst the above definition, on its face, appears to be straightforward, there are some ambiguities in practice; and in actual fact, personal data has been given a much narrower ambit in its interpretation by the judiciary in Hong Kong than its literal meaning affords.

For instance, in relation to the criterion in (a) (the "relatedness criterion"), the privacy commissioner has ruled that a relationship must be important and not trivial so as to avoid an absurd outcome from taking a literal view of this requirement.[27] In arriving at this conclusion, the privacy commissioner has acknowledged that "… [f]rom a plain reading of the section, it is perhaps difficult to infer a strict requirement in paragraph (a) that the relationship in question must be important, rather than trivial."[28]

Besides narrowing the definition of personal data, the PDPO also further narrowed the application of the PDPO and effectively the ambit of what constitutes personal data as a result of adopting a subjective test of what constitutes collection of personal data. In the Eastweek case,[29] in a 2001 Court of Appeal decision, the court held that it is not a collection of personal data where a person collects data of an unidentified individual with no intention to identify that individual. Accordingly, Hong Kong now has a much narrower focus as regards the ambit of data protection when compared to other jurisdictions, notwithstanding its adoption of a principle-based (as opposed to prescriptive) approach to data protection.

In the opinion of the PCPD,[30] the position taken by the Court of Appeal in the Eastweek case is confined to the facts of that case where the identity of the woman was not collected, but rather aspects of her appearance and dress were collected. As such, for example, if a person's identity is the subject of a collection but subsequently not the objective or purpose of the collection, it may well be that that would constitute personal data. It was also stressed that the case is confined to its facts and should not be read as carte blanche for the collection of personal data based ostensibly on other purposes or for reasons other than a person's identity.

Nevertheless, this approach, which incorporates an "intention to identify" proviso, remains law and is an example of the reasonably practicable approach to interpreting the scope of personal data.[31] Hence, how a person's data is collected, used, or shared and the objective of the data management as well as the communication of that objective can have an effect on whether it can be made to fall outside the scope of personal data and the application of the Act. Also, from this view, the relatedness criterion and the identifiability factor are separate and disjunctive requirements for a violation of the PDPO obligations.

In another case,[32] the Court of Appeal ruled that the minutes of a meeting containing the complainant's name are not his personal data. On the interpretation of what is "practicable," examples were given in a Court of First Instance judgement as to when that is the case in relation to access to information.[33] Basically, it does not mean that it has to be impossible, but is a standard that is below that, which is reasonable (ostensibly from the perspective of the data user or collector), although the line is not clearly defined and remains to be determined in accordance with the facts of each case. It should be noted that the "practicable" test is built into the definition of "personal data" and as such it actually determines whether personal information is personal data for the purposes of the PDPO or otherwise. That is, "personal data" is a legal construct and does not necessarily cover what a layman may consider personal information or data.

What is the general approach, and the test used, to determine personal data[34] and issues such as of fairness, and how does the Hong Kong Privacy Ordinance (2013) approach its privacy goals vis-à-vis other (sometimes competing) interests? The PDPO stressed that the cases are confined to the facts and cannot be taken to indicate a view towards personal data that is "subjective." However, the approach is effectively not based on human rights and privacy; rather, the courts (and the PDPO) have taken a nuanced approach by balancing the interests of various stakeholders regarding personal data.

Some final notes on this matter may be of interest: Hong Kong has a similar practical approach to the matter of seeking consent, which is akin to how the PDPA deemed consent provision. It also seems to operate like an "opt-out" type of system, since notice upon collection means that the subject is given knowledge and can decide to retract permission or, in another manner, restrict or control the use of personal information. The focus is also on the implementation of the six data protection principles in a "fair" and, as such, practicable method, under the circumstances of each case. There are also specific exemptions within the body of the Act itself, like those that Singapore has in the Schedules to its PDPA. Finally, the PDPO applies to public as well and private entities, and the assessment of the PDPO is that the government is generally doing well in terms of compliance with the Ordinance. The use of personal data in the public domain is also interesting and unlike the approach in Singapore, where personal information in the public domain is exempted from the consent requirement.[35]

The PDPO has been amended from time to time. This is of interest to note if subsequent data economy studies are done with a view to the use of personal information, whether for individual consumer assessment alone and/or for direct marketing. On the latter, is should be noted that the current focus of the PDPO (and the PCPD) is on direct marketing through the use of personal data.[36] A new Part 6 (Sections 35A–M) deals with direct marketing using personal data in a manner that is more comprehensive and that relates to a wider array of media and purposes than the DNC regime in Singapore.

The PCPD is independent of the government. Nevertheless, it is attuned to the various interests and stakeholders of personal data as well as the government policy towards it, including the drive towards being a smart city.[37] As was noted above, the approach is one of balancing the interests of stakeholders in Hong Kong society in relation to personal data, rather than the paramount concern with personal or individual privacy over all else, including economic interests. This is apparent from the latest focus on the level of fairness of direct marketing practices and the guidelines relating to it. The PCPD is aware of the special relationship that the SAR has with China and of their differences in policy and laws in relation to data privacy that may be problematic if, for example, personal data is requested or collected by a mainland entity. However, the problem has not yet arisen to a level that is a cause for concern for them.

Taiwan

Taiwan has one of the oldest data protection regimes in Asia. From 1995 to 2012, data protection in Taiwan was governed by the Computer Processed Personal Data Protection Act, which was heavily influenced by the OECD Privacy Guidelines. In 2010, as part of measures to reform data protection in Taiwan in order to bring it up to modern standards, especially as it relates to data protection issues that have emerged with the increasing ubiquity of the Internet, Taiwan enacted the Personal Information Protection Act (TW PIPA).

However, the TW PIPA did not come into force until 1 October 2012, as the TW PIPA faced significant pushback from among other stakeholders such as the financial industry due to:

1. The stringent notification requirement for personal information currently held (Article 54);

2. The limited exceptions to the consensual use of sensitive personal data (Article 6); and
3. Criminal liabilities that arise from the misuse of personal data even when such misuse is incidental and not for profit (Article 41).

Consequently, even though the TW PIPA came into force in October 2012, Articles 54 and 6 were not brought into force, as the Executive Yuan took the view that these articles were administratively impractical. That Article 41 was given effect was also not without controversy. However, this tension was eventually resolved in 2016 when the Legislative Yuan passed an amendment to the TW PIPA to relax the conditions under Articles 6 and 54. In this regard, it should be noted that the TW PIPA applies to entities in both the public and private sectors.

Notwithstanding the relatively comprehensive data protection legislation in the TW PIPA, there is also strong protection for individual privacy and data protection as a dimension of privacy under the Constitution of Taiwan. Specifically, the Council of Grand Justices, Taiwan's top constitutional court, has over the years developed the constitutional status of privacy and made it clear that both privacy and data protection (expressed as information self-determination) are integral features of the Taiwanese Constitution.

In this regard, in a 2004 decision, the Council stated:

> The right of privacy, though not clearly enumerated under the Constitution, is an indispensable fundamental right protected under Article 22 of the Constitution because it is necessary to preserve human dignity, individuality, and the wholeness of personality development, as well as to safeguard the freedom of private living space from interference and the freedom of self-control of personal information. Where the investigation power exercised by the Legislative Yuan may involve any restrictions imposed on the fundamental rights of the people, not only should there be a basis of law whose contents should be clear and definite, but it should also follow the principles of proportionality and due process of law.[38]

In 2005, this was reinforced by the Council when it considered the constitutional status of compulsory fingerprinting for identity cards and stated:

> To preserve human dignity and to respect free development of personality is the core value of the constitutional structure of free democracy. Although the right of privacy is not among those rights specifically enumerated in the Constitution, it should nonetheless be considered as an indispensable fundamental right and thus

protected under Article 22 of the Constitution for purposes of pre-serving human dignity, individuality and moral integrity, as well as preventing invasions of personal privacy and maintaining self-control of personal information. As far as the right of information privacy is concerned, which regards the self-control of personal information, it is intended to guarantee that the people have the right to decide whether or not to disclose their personal information, and, if so, to what extent, at what time, in what manner and to which people such information will be disclosed. It is also designed to guarantee that the people have the right to know and control how their personal information will be used, as well as the right to correct any inaccurate entries contained in their information.[39]

Besides the protection afforded by the Constitution, private protection for an individual's privacy is also provided under Taiwanese law as, since 1999, the Civil Code in Taiwan has provided for a privacy tort by way of the introduction of Article 195, which states:

> If a person has wrongfully committed damage to the body, health, reputation, liberty, credit, privacy or chastity of another, or to another's personality in severe ways the injured person may claim a reasonable compensation in money even if such injury is not a purely pecuniary loss. If it was reputation that has been damaged the injured person may also claim the taking of proper measures for the rehabilitation of his reputation.

Under the TW PIPA, "personal information" is defined as a natural person's name, date of birth, national unified ID card number, passport number, special features, fingerprint, marital status, family background, educational background, occupation, contact information, financial status, social activities, sensitive personal information, and any other information that may be used to directly or indirectly identify a natural person.

Sensitive personal information – a relatively new concept introduced by an amendment to the TW PIPA in December 2015 and that came into force in March 2016 – relates to medical history, medical treatments, genealogy, sex life, health check results, and criminal records.

Korea

In South Korea, the Personal Information Protection Act (SK PIPA) that was promulgated in 2011 entered into force on 30 September 2011. Prior to the SK PIPA, there was no comprehensive data protection law in South

Korea, and today data protection, where it is available, is governed by specific sectorial legislation. Specifically, these legislation are:

1. The Act on Promotion of Information and Communication Network Utilisation and Information Protection ("IT Network Act"), which regulates the collection and use of personal information by IT service providers;
2. The Use and Protection of Credit Information Act, which regulates the use and disclosure of personal credit information, defined as credit information that is necessary to determine the credit rating, credit transaction capacity, etc., of an individual person; and
3. The Act on Real Name Financial Transactions and Guarantee of Secrecy ("ARNFTGS"), which applies to information obtained by financial or financial services institutions.

With the entry into force of the SK PIPA, such sectorial legislation continues to apply, as the SK PIPA expressly yields to sectorial legislation where it is present, but applies generally otherwise, and this is in relation to entities in both the public and private sectors.

Privacy in South Korea is constitutionally protected, and there are three articles in the South Korea Constitution that specifically cater to privacy. These are:

1. Article 16, which states that "All citizens shall be free from intrusion into their place of residence. In case of search or seizure in a residence, a warrant issued by a judge upon request of a prosecutor shall be presented";
2. Article 17, which states that "the privacy of no citizen shall be infringed"; and
3. Article 18, which states that "The privacy of correspondence of no citizen shall be infringed."

In view of these express constitutional safeguards, courts in South Korea have taken a very robust view of privacy. In 2003, in a decision that outlawed unlawful access to and abuse of personal information, the Constitutional Court stated:

> The right to privacy is a fundamental right which prevents the state from looking into the private life of citizens, and provides for the protection from the state's intervention or prohibition of free conduct of private living. Concretely, the privacy protection is defined as protecting and maintaining the confidential secrecy of an individual; ensuring the

inviolability of one's own private life; keeping from other's intervention of such sensitive areas as one's conscience or sexual life; holding in esteem one's own personality and emotional life; and preserving one's mental inner world.[40]

In 2005, the Constitutional Court went even further and equated data protection as falling under the ambit of privacy when it pronounced:

> The right to control one's own personal information is a right of the subject of the information to personally decide when, to whom or by whom, and to what extent his or her information will be disclosed or used. It is a basic right, although not specified in the Constitution, existing to protect the personal freedom of decision from the risk caused by the enlargement of state functions and info-communication technology.[41]

More recently, the Constitutional Court also struck out the Limited Identity Verification System Statute in 2012 that requires Internet users to use their real names online as unconstitutional, as it viewed that there were no substantial gains in requiring the use of real names that justify the restrictions on the individual's right to free speech and privacy.[42]

Under Article 2 of PIPA and the IT Network Act, "personal information" means information pertaining to a living individual, which contains information identifying a specific person with a name, a national ID number, images, or other similar information (including information that does not, by itself, make it possible to identify a specific person, but enables the recipient of the information to easily identify such a person if combined with other information).

Notwithstanding an identical definition of personal information, there is an important difference between the SK PIPA and the IT Network Act, as the latter only regulates the personal information of users. Under the SK PIPA and the IT Network Act, there is also a concept of sensitive personal information, and this is defined as personal information consisting of information relating to a living individual's:

1. Thoughts or creed;
2. History regarding membership in a political party or labour union;
3. Political views;
4. Healthcare and sexual life; and
5. Other personal information stipulated under the Enforcement Decree (the Presidential Decree) of the PIPA that is anticipated to otherwise intrude seriously upon the privacy of the person.

In terms of exclusion, PIPA excludes personal information that falls under the following categories:

1. Personal information handled by public agencies that was collected under the Statistics Act;
2. Personal information that was collected or requested for the purpose of conducting an analysis related to national security;
3. Personal information that is temporarily processed due to an urgent need based on public safety and welfare concerns, such as public hygiene; and
4. Personal information that is collected and/or used by the media (for news collecting and reporting), religious organisations (for missionary work), and political parties (for the nomination of a candidate in an election).

In contrast, there are no exclusions under the IT Network Act.

Japan

The emergence of data protection in Japan came on the back of popular discomfort with the government's plan to introduce a national electronic network to record an individual's residence and movement therein within Japan. Specifically, the genesis of the data protection legislation in Japan was a compromise struck by the then ruling Liberal Democratic Party, which, in its desire to enact the Basic Resident Registers Act 1999, offered checks and balances in the form of data protection legislation to assuage the public's concern about the misuse of such personal data.

Consequently, three main laws were enacted to deal with the protection of personal information on 30 May 2003. These are:

1. Act on the Protection of Personal Information (APPI);
2. Act on the Protection of Personal Information Held by Administrative Organs; and
3. Act on the Protection of Personal Information Held by Independent Administrative Agencies.

Of the three, the APPI is the key legislation, and it sets out the basic data protection principles as they relate to entities in both the public and private sector.

Under Article 13 of the Constitution of Japan:

All of the people shall be respected as individuals. The right to life, liberty, and the pursuit of happiness shall, to the extent that it does not interfere with the public welfare, be the supreme consideration in legislation and in other governmental affairs.

Stemming from this, Japanese courts have established that there is a right of privacy for individuals and that there is a right of persons to their private lives and this is not to be disclosed except for with a legitimate reason. In other words, privacy in Japan is construed as the right to control one's own personal information. Therefore, in addition to the APPI, the personal information of individuals is also protected under the Constitution of Japan by privacy rights.

Besides the APPI and the Constitution, there are also specific laws that deal with privacy in a sectorial context. For instance, under Article 4 of the Telecommunications Business Law, no person may infringe on the privacy of the communications handled by telecommunications business operators.

Within the context of the APPI, the relevant analogue to the conventional understanding of personal data is personal information. Specifically, personal information is defined at Article 2, Paragraph 1 of the APPI as:

> … information about a living individual which can identify the specific individual by name, date of birth or other description contained in such information (including such information as will allow easy reference to other information and will thereby enable the identification of the specific individual).

In this regard, personal information should not be confused with personal data, which is defined under the APPI at Article 2, Paragraph 6 as meaning personal information constituting a personal information database. A personal information database is in turn defined at Article 2, Paragraph 6 of the APPI as:

1. An assembly of information systematically arranged in such a way that specific personal information can be retrieved by a computer; and
2. An assembly of information designated by a Cabinet Order as being systematically arranged in such a way that specific personal information can be easily retrieved.

However, it should be noted that with the amendment of the APPI in 2015, Article 2, Paragraph 4 specifically provides that where the use of any assembly of information is not likely to harm the interests of the individual principals, such an assembly of information will not fall within the definition of a personal information database.

Finally, the amended APPI also added a new category of "sensitive personal data," which refers to a person's race, beliefs, social status, medical history, criminal record, whether one has been a victim of crime, and other personal information that needs careful handling so as not to cause social discrimination, prejudice, or other disadvantages. The details of sensitive personal data are, however, still not settled as the ordinance of the amended APPI, which clarifies the necessary designation, has yet to be issued.

The EU

The EU generally (and the European group of nations) was the earliest proponent of data privacy rights and remains ahead of the curve in setting increasingly high standards of privacy laws and data protection obligations, both at the EU level as well as at the national level. The EU Data Protection Directive (95/46/EC) on the protection of individuals with regards to the processing of personal data and on the free movement of such data was adopted in 1995 and served as an important pillar to the EU's privacy rights and human rights body of laws. Due to the nature of a Directive, the implementation of its principles, which largely reflect the OECD principles as noted above, was not as consistent as privacy and data protection proponents would have liked, although it remains generally strong across Europe and, in particular, within the member states themselves. The GDPR (2016/679) on the protection of natural persons with regards to the processing of personal data and on the free movement of such data, which repeals and replaces the Directive and was adopted on 27 April 2016 and began implementation from 25 May 2018, strengthens the data privacy regime in its member states in two ways: first, it is directly applicable and has direct effect on – and hence is immediately enforceable as law in – member states. Second, the Regulation further raises the standards of compliance from its predecessor and introduces new data privacy concepts.

The GDPR applies to both the "data controller," which is an organisation that deals with data relating to EU residents or a data subject based in the EU, as well as the "data processor," which is an organisation that processes the data for a data controller. Although the data controller remains responsible for the data and for compliance with GDPR obligations, even in the possession of a designated data processor, the data processor is also obligated under the Regulation to comply with obligations such as breach reporting, security, and protection requirements.

What are of relevance in the context of the type of study conducted in this book, and noteworthy for this purpose, are as follows:

1. Legal analytics, including the use of AI for that function, which profiles individuals based on their decision-making and behaviour, can be contested under Article 15 of the GDPR. Hence, for example, a data subject can challenge significant decisions that have an effect on them that are made based on technical methods (e.g. the use of algorithms) and other forms of assessment. Article 22(1) of the Regulation states that, except for certain exceptions such as the presence of explicit consent, "data subject[s] have the right not to be subject to a decision based solely on automated processing, including profiling, which produces legal effects concerning him or her or [that] similarly significantly affect him or her."

2. The data controller must implement measures that meet the "privacy by design" and "privacy by default" principles under Article 25 of the GDPR, which requires greater effort and cost for organisations to implement data protection measures by weaving them into their business processes for products and services.

3. There is also a trend, as shown by the GDPR, towards auditing, data breach reporting, and stronger security requirements, as well as the obligation to erase personal data under the "right to be forgotten" principle. These are still not common requirements in Asian countries, especially the data breach reporting and auditing obligations, but they may feature in future amendments. In relation to the former, Article 35 of the Regulation provides for data protection impact assessments to be conducted in response to certain risks to the rights of data subjects and also for mitigation measures. There are also strong administrative requirements such as for the appointment of DPOs, contact points, and processes within organisations generally.

4. The Regulation (and most data protection regimes) does not provide a blanket exemption for public agencies, unlike in Singapore, and the exceptions to the basic requirements of consent and notification are narrower than in most other jurisdictions and in Singapore. In particular, the standard of obtaining consent is high. Consent must be explicitly obtained ("by a statement or clear affirmative action") and it must be clearly and freely given (e.g. not subject to unnecessary conditions or coerced, and it must be unambiguous). There are also even more stringent requirements when collecting and dealing with the personal data of special classes or categories of persons that are identified as vulnerable and that require greater protection, such as children.

5. The GDPR also provides for the options of data anonymisation and pseudonymisation, the latter of which is the transformation of personal data in a manner that does not allow for the attribution of the resulting data to specific data subjects without the use of additional information (e.g. by encryption or tokenisation). Safeguards must be put in place to prevent breaches or leaks.

It should be noted that these obligations do not apply if the data subject is confined to non-EU residents or data subjects. However, future developments and enhancements to the data protection laws in the region and in Singapore may bring in some of these concepts, so it is important to be aware of their effects on and implications for such studies. Moreover, if future studies involve the collection, use, and disclosure of personal data of non-Singaporeans, such as Europeans, this data does fall under the GDPR for legal consideration due to its extra-territorial scope, and as such, the treatment of such data should meet the (often higher) standards of the jurisdiction concerned to avoid risks of penalties and fines, as well as the threat of data flow restrictions imposed by the jurisdictions concerned. The risk of sanctions may not be high, but there should nevertheless be an awareness of such risks and obligations.

Asian data protection developments and experiences with use of data collected from cashless smart cards

The ez-link card is the main card used for transport payment in Singapore. It can be used on various modes of public transport, including the most popular and widely used services of buses and MRT trains. The ez-link card is also used for other purposes, including payment under the electronic road pricing system and at car parks fitted with EZ-Link's electronic payment system (EPS), as well as payment for purchases at select retail outlets and for government services and fines.

The conventional ez-link card is like a "Visa payWave" and is "contactless" as it does not require swiping of the card. The EZ-Link mobile app automates payment by charging to a user-designated Visa or MasterCard debit or credit card. Users must first enter personal and payment details into the app before they can tap their ez-link card on the smart phone to top up the card.

With the new near-field communication SIM card, certain mobile devices can be used for payments on MRT, LRT, and public buses, as well as at more than 30,000 ez-link acceptance points across Singapore, according to a joint press release by LTA, Infocomm Development Authority of Singapore (IDA), and EZ-Link on 29 March 2016.[43] Its popularity and use remain to be determined.

Hong Kong

The Octopus card is the equivalent of the Singapore ez-link card in Hong Kong. It has a deep penetration of the payments market, and its uses, like for the ez-link card, extend beyond payment for public transportation.

The company has issued different versions of the card. The concession cards are offered to students whose personal data relevant to their eligibility to the card (e.g. age and enrolment) is collected and used for that purpose. There is no special concession card for the elderly or seniors, although such cards can be obtained at MTR stations. The safeguard against abuse is through checks by inspectors at stations. Where cards are linked to bank accounts for topping up, personal information necessary for that, such as account numbers, is collected and used for that purpose. The Octopus card is also used for other purposes, such as payment for goods and so on, much like the ez-link card in Singapore.

The following is an account of the Octopus card incident that involved data breach and a violation of the PDPO in 2010:

> Octopus operated a customer reward programme whereby registered members could earn Reward Dollars for making purchases from Octopus' business partners by presenting the Octopus card. The Reward Dollars earned may be redeemed for goods and services from the business partners. Since March 2010, subscribers for the programme started to complain about Octopus' transfer of their personal data to third parties for direct marketing purposes without their knowledge or consent.[44]
>
> First, the notice informing the customers of the purpose of the use of the personal data collected, and the classes of persons to whom the data would be transferred, was poorly laid out and presented. For example, the font size used for the notice was so small (about 1mm × 1mm in English) that people with normal eyesight would find the words difficult to read unless aided by a magnifying glass. Second, the purpose of use of personal data and classes of data transferees were couched in liberal and vague terms. It would not be practicable for customers to ascertain with a reasonable degree of certainty how their personal data could be used and who could have the use of them. Third, Octopus had, without the customers' explicit consent, transferred their personal data to a number of partner companies for marketing the latter's products and services. Octopus played little or no part in the marketing process. But it received monetary gains from the partner companies as a reward for the data transfer. The transaction in essence was sale of personal data. Finally, under prior agreement with Octopus, one partner company promoted its products and services by calling Octopus' customers in the name of Octopus. In effect, the customers have been deceived as regards the identity of the caller.[45]

The Octopus card suffered a loss of public trust and damage to its corporate image. After an investigation and a finding of violations of the Act, and due to the restrictions on punitive actions that the Privacy Commissioner could take under the PDPO at that time, it was determined that no offence had occurred, but that the Commissioner could serve an enforcement notice to the company to direct Octopus to take remedial steps within a specified period in the event that contravention was continuing or likely to be continued or repeated.[46] Since that incident, Octopus management sought to restore public trust and avoid legal sanctions by putting in place measures and protocols in relation to personal data. The incident also prompted new PCPD guidelines to be issued and amendments to the Act to be made on direct marketing several years later. The Octopus card is currently generally in compliance with the PDPO.

There are many other instances of data breaches, most of which are straightforward, and several such cases heard by the administrative appeals board and courts can be found on the PCPD website.[47]

Taiwan

Taiwan is an interesting case study as the Cross Border Combi Card for transport and payment, such as for admission to attractions and retail purchases, is in the works between Singapore's ez-link and EasyCard in Taiwan.[48] Taiwan also has a large number of contactless card users, including users of EasyCard and iPass, and is also showing increasing use of contactless cards issued by banks. Taiwan also has an e-city initiative that is similar to Singapore and Hong Kong's race towards a smart nation, and given its size, it is also comparable to both countries in terms of the effort needed to meet such a goal.

Korea and Japan

South Korea and Japan are important to any study regarding the future of contactless transactions, including transport and transactional payments, as they are the technological innovators and leaders in Asia. Also, South Korea and Japan have some of the most advanced (and complicated) transport systems today. Furthermore, as noted above, both countries have relatively advanced data protection laws compared to other parts of Asia.

In Korea, the Upass is issued by the Seoul Bus Transport Association as a prepaid card for the transport system in the city. T-money ("T" stands for travel, touch, traffic, and technology), rechargeable cards, and other smart devices are also used for payment of transport fares and the purchase of goods and services from some businesses in Seoul and beyond. T-money is available on the Internet and on mobile platforms, as well as in physical card form, such as the Seoul City and City Pass Plus card. Outside the city, Cash Bee is used and serves many of the same functions.

Japan has one of the most advanced and efficient transportation networks in the world, as well as one of the most complicated, with a network of transport options operated by many different companies. Japan also has a large contactless card market for its Suica/Pasmo cards, other cards used by different transport systems or in different regions, and related devices. The FeliCa contactless radiofrequency identification (RFID) smart card system, for example, is the same as the one used in the Octopus card in Hong Kong. It was reported in 2013 that Japan Rail (JR) had announced plans to sell marketing reports based on data gathered from Suica users such as travel patterns (tap-in and tap-out data), age, gender, and time of use. The data disclosed would be anonymised to follow the Act on the Protection of Personal Information. Due to the fear that personal data could be collected and used for other purposes, particularly data relating to purchasing habits and patterns, JR provides an opt-out procedure in relation to such data handling.[49]

United Kingdom

The Oyster card is a contactless smart card produced and co-operated by Cubic Transportation Systems, a subsidiary of the US company Cubic Corporation. It is a leading integrator of intelligent travel applications, providing contactless smart card technology products and services. It is involved in a vast number of fare collection projects across jurisdictions including the USA, the UK, Australia, Canada, and some European countries. The Oyster card is used for electronic payment of public transport fees by commuters in London on most of its public transport platforms. It has been operating since 2003 in London, and the range of its uses has expanded over time, like the cards in other countries such as Singapore and Hong Kong, to now include use in payment for other products and services. It provides many options, including functioning as a season ticket and for pay-as-you-go uses. In addition, as with other such cards, concession and visitor cards are also issued. Interestingly, for free or discounted cards, the image of the eligible user (e.g. students, under-16s and over-60s, and the disabled) is printed on the card.

The Oyster card can provide full anonymity or be registered, such as for verification purposes (for online sale and purchase of products with the card) and for additional services including protection from loss and theft, auto-top-ups, as well as for the provision of after-sales services. The Oyster card function has also been tied to credit cards through Barclaycard, a major credit card issuer. The shift is now towards contactless payment card systems, including credit and debit card options.

Each Oyster card bears unique numerical identifiers, and limited usage data is stored in the card itself, while movement and transaction data is collected by Transport for London and stored for up to eight weeks before it is disassociated from the card.

Although there have been criticisms that the data it collects and stores centrally can be a threat to the personal data privacy interests of its users, there have not been any reported major incidents of data breach or misuse. Most use of the data collected has been kept within the purpose of collection, such as identification for special treatment and discounts or concessions, and also within the terms of agreement, which constitute notification and the consent of the users concerned. Outside access has mainly been sought, and only been provided, to the police for investigative purposes and pursuant to the law.

Arguments for a facilitative regime of data analytics for a data economy

Singapore intends to become the foremost data economy hub. Hence, she must take a facilitative policy approach and provide a permissive framework, but in a manner that maintains baseline protections (particularly safeguards such as cybersecurity to protect against leakage of such information) for personal data. There is a way to reconcile both objectives even if there may be tensions in certain areas, in a manner consistent with the objectives of the PDPA as stated in Section 3 of the Act. Moreover, to do so will not only be consistent with global and regional standards, but also maintain her integrity as a serious global and Asian standard-bearer of data protection.

General data analytics

This involves examining data in the abstract, involving people in groups that are large enough to be unidentifiable and whose individuality or identity is not the focus of the research and study. This is in fact the approach taken in this study. Aggregated data that does not identify or have an individual as its focus does not require the organisation concerned to comply with the PDPA, provided that the data is obtained from legitimate sources and is collected, used, or disclosed in a manner that in no way involves personal and personally identifiable data.

Specific data analytics (descriptive metadata)

This covers the study of groups of people as well as individual traits or behaviours for the purpose of targeted treatment – whether for services or marketing outreach. For example, student and senior concession cards and the collection of the personal information contained therein, including location tools, can be useful to track the location of the individual concerned.

This can be useful for social objectives, such as detecting the location of seniors with dementia or memory loss, those who are at risk of becoming lost, or children who may have run away from home or have been kidnapped.

For the average adult, it can also be useful for automatic top-ups (financial information), an operation that is already being used by financial institutions. It can also be used for direct marketing campaigns through behavioural analysis and so on. It is more likely that this will be an objective of a data economy study of the monetisation of data or for any number of smart nation initiatives, including the streamlining of services and the efficient use of resources.

Use of personal data for direct advertising and marketing

As noted above, the use of personal data for personal profiling, tracking of physical movement or online surfing habits and location information, and the use of personal data (including personal contact information) for direct advertising and marketing are likely goals of a data economy study. As such, it will be interesting to use a jurisdictional example to illustrate the legal challenges and considerations that are pertinent to the matter. The example used here will be Hong Kong, in relation to the use of personal data for direct marketing purposes.

Hong Kong

As noted above, Hong Kong is a good example of the direction that data economy studies can take and the objectives that the outcomes of such studies can and are likely to achieve. Because of the prominent use of personal data for direct or targeted marketing via various online platforms, including websites and through voice, text, and electronic mail messages, the current legislative developments have been to calibrate a fair and reasonable direct marketing regime under the PDPO.

Hong Kong's regulation and enforcement relating to direct marketing and the use of the personal data of individuals by organisations in relation to economic interests, both as a currency for data analytics and as a tool in targeted marketing, have become prominent features of its approach. Law reform has also focused on more stringent measures to regulate direct marketing behaviour since the widely reported cases of abuse in 2010 by the Octopus operator. The PCPD also actively publishes guidelines and updates.

The Amendment Ordinance to the PDPO, aimed at enhancing the protection of the personal data of individuals, is a direct result of the increase in incidents of data privacy breaches in Hong Kong, particularly the Octopus card incident. The Amendment Ordinance introduced several changes; in particular, and relevant to this part, are new provisions provided for tighter restrictions on the use of personal data in direct marketing. Other amendments included stronger enforcement measures and higher penalties.

In particular, the new law on direct marketing requires businesses to adopt an "opt-in" approach to obtaining an individual's consent before they can send advertisements or marketing materials to them. This can come in the form of an explicit "indication of no objection" (as defined in the PDPO).

As this data economy study is intended to eventually lead to the sharing of data for the purposes of business strategy, including retail and marketing, these changes are of interest in order to anticipate the potential issues and problems under current and projected changes in society and the law.

Suggestions for future studies

This study has shown that future research in this area should set out the outcomes it seeks to achieve and the intended recipients of the data output in terms of their interest, purpose, and the utility of the data. Assessment should be done at the data analytics or processing stage and at the data-sharing or disclosure and dissemination stage to detect any personal data as falling under the existing DP and, where appropriate, DNC regimes. If it does, a legal liability and risk assessment study should be conducted early in the agenda. If a research study of this nature is projected to be achieved over a span of time and is ambitious enough, ongoing tracking of proposed changes to the PDPA should also be done, together with potential amendments to the Act, in a manner that is facilitative, or at least not an impediment, to the study concerned. In relation to this, constant feedback to lawmakers, and possibly lobbying, will probably be required to ensure an accommodating environment through which actionable outcomes can be attained.

In the meantime, it should be noted that the 2018 proposed amendments to the PDPA do include mandatory data breach reporting. Such reporting obligations to affected persons and to the PDPC are likely to be required in relation to data breaches that pose risk of impact or harm to individuals, and to the PDPC only where the breach is significant. It should be noted that mandatory data breach reporting and security measures will also feature in the new Singapore Cybersecurity Act of 2018 that deals with data that falls under the scope of the "critical information infrastructure," and some of this data may overlap with personal data under the PDPA. Conversely, there is additional room to manoeuvre when it comes to the consent requirement, as additional exceptions based on the legality or legitimate business purpose of use and where notification of purpose will suffice, provided that certain safeguards and conditions are met, will likely be included in the Act.

The renewed focus on the ethical consideration and legality of data analytics due to the Cambridge Analytica–Facebook data breach incident in relation to consent and notification requirements, as well as the robustness of data-sharing restrictions and security measures, means that stronger legal protections and ethical guidelines as well as their implementation can be expected in the future. Already, Internet intermediaries such as search engines like Google and media platforms like Facebook are revising their privacy policies and the privacy by design/default measures in their functions.

Notes

1 Acquisti, Alessandro, "The Economics and Behavioral Economics of Privacy." In: J. Lane et al., *Privacy, Big Data, and the Public Good*, Cambridge University Press, New York, 2014, p. 81.
2 Section 2 of the PDPA.
3 Personal Data Protection (Statutory Bodies) Notification S 149/2013.
4 For example, reading intention or reasonable effort into the collection and use obligation of what is otherwise strictly personal and/or identifiable data can reduce the scope of the Act. On this, one can compare the Hong Kong approach to what is potentially the Singapore approach.
5 Section 11 of the PDPA.
6 Section 18 of the PDPA.
7 Section 20 of the PDPA. The reasonableness test (and in some cases the practicableness test) is variously used in the other provisions on specific obligations such as the obligations to provide an individual with access to their personal data, to correct that data, to main the accuracy of personal data, and finally to guide organisations on how much protection or security is required and how long they can retain personal data.
8 Section 17 read with Schedules 2–4 of the PDPA. Schedules 5 and 6 also provide for exceptions from the access and correction requirements under the Act.
9 Section 3 of the PDPA.
10 Chik, Warren & Keep Ying Joey Pang, "The Meaning and Scope of Personal Data Under the Singapore Personal Data Protection Act," *Signapore Academy of Law Journal*, 2014, 26:354–397.
11 The reason for such caution is that, unlike in Hong Kong, Singapore's PDPA contains generous general exclusions and detailed partial exemptions from the application of the Act, and as such, a wider and more generous interpretation of "personal data" to offset those carve-outs (and also the reasonableness standard of compliance throughout the Act) may be justified. See Chik & Pang at pp. 366–371.
12 Generally excluded under Section 4(1)(c) from and in relation to the collection, use, or disclosure of personal data.

13 In excluding public agencies from the purview of the PDPA, the government justified and assured the public that its internal standards of protection and measures of compliance will not be lesser than that set by the Act for private organisations.

14 As noted, the "reasonableness test" is the standard set for almost all the principles and obligations under the Act, including the general compliance provision, which states that "[i]n meeting its responsibilities under this Act, an organisation shall consider what a reasonable person would consider appropriate in the circumstances" (Section 11[1]). It also appears in the purpose provision (Section 3). How it is applies varies according to the context and the obligation concerned.

15 Infra. This means that if the primary purpose was not to focus on the individual person (and his/her identity), but on other matters such as the fashion, event, or background (i.e. the "wider picture"), then it is not personal data.

16 The Anonymization ToolBox from the University of Dallas was referenced. See: www.cs.utdallas.edu/dspl/cgi-bin/toolbox/index.php.

17 See Second Schedule 1(c), Third Schedule 1(c), and Fourth Schedule 1(d) of the PDPA, respectively. "Publicly available" is defined under Section 2 of the PDPA.

18 Other data that may require individualised assessment include tracking the movement or location data of certain individuals such as the elderly, disabled, or criminals, or tracking the surfing and spending habits of individuals online for marketing purposes, etc.

19 At 1(f) of the Schedule.

20 At 1(f) and (i) of the Schedule.

21 At 1(h) and (q) of the Schedule.

22 At 2 of the Third Schedule and 4 of the Fourth Schedule, the conditions for the research purpose to apply for exemption from seeking consent is contingent on several factors, including (and notably) proof that: "the research purpose cannot reasonably be accomplished without the personal data being provided in an individually identifiable form"; "it is impracticable for the organisation to seek the consent of the individual for the disclosure"; "the benefits to be derived from the linkage are clearly in the public interest"; and that security, confidentiality, retention, and notification/purpose requirements of the recipient of such information down the data supply/sharing chain (in relation to the obligations relating to disclosure only) are observed.

23 TransitLink's Data Protection Policy, available at: www.transitlink.com.sg/Aboutus.aspx?Id=7.

24 This is featured in the 2015–2016 annual report of the PCPD, available at: www.pcpd.org.hk/english/resources_centre/publications/annual_report/annualreport2016.html.

25 Article 29 of the Basic Law.

26 Article 30 of the Basic Law.

27 *AAB No. 49/2001* and *AAB No. 14/2007.*

28 *Data Protection Principles in the Personal Data (Privacy) Ordinance – From the Privacy Commissioner's Perspective* (2nd Edition), at p. 10.

29 "Eastweek Publisher Limited & Another v Privacy Commissioner for Personal Data," *Hong Kong Law Reports & Digest*, 2000, 2:83.

30 These are the opinions of the PCPD provided to the author on a visit to the PCPD Office on 16 January 2017. It should be noted that these views are not necessarily the legal position that will be taken by the courts of legislature if clarifications are made in the future.

31 Section 2 defines "practicable" as "reasonably practicable."

32 Hong Kong Court of Appeal case CACV 960/2000 at pp. 6–8, available at: www.pcpd.org.hk/english/enforcement/judgments/files/CACV000960_2000.pdf (Chinese version only). This case may be compared to other cases, such as the UK *Edem* case, regarding the treatment of personal information within the body of a document that also contains other data that may or may not be relevant to the complainant concerned (and that may relate to competing interests, whether or not relating to the personal data of others).

33 Hong Kong Court of First Instance case HCAL 1050/2000 at pp. 18–23, available at: http://legalref.judiciary.gov.hk/lrs/common/search/search_result_detail_frame.jsp?DIS=27638&QS=%2B&TP=JU (Chinese version only).

34 Information must "relate to" a living person directly or indirectly, can be used "practically" "to identify" that person (directly or indirectly ascertained), and that exists in a form for "practicable" access or processing. "Practicable" is defined as "reasonably practicable" (Section 2, PO) and the reference to both "reasonableness" and "practicality" as a test is included in the Singapore PDPA as well. Hence, it may well be of interest to reference how these standards are set in the Hong Kong context.

35 See PCPD Office, Hong Kong, *Guidance Note: Guidance on Use of Personal Data Obtained from the Public Domain* (August 2013), available at: www.cityu.edu.hk/vpad/public_domain_e.pdf.

36 The PCPD issued a new Guidance Note on new provisions relating to direct marketing in January 2013 and the amended provisions relating to it took effect on 1 April 2013. See PCPD Office, Hong Kong, *Guidance Note: New Guidance on Direct Marketing* (January 2013), available at: www.pcpd.org.hk/english/publications/files/GN_DM_e.pdf.

37 See Privacy Commissioner for Personal Data, Hong Kong, *2015–2016 Annual Report: Smart City Data Protection*, available at: www.pcpd.org.hk/english/resources_centre/publications/annual_report/annualreport2016.html.

38 Council of Grand Justices, "319 Shooting Decision": "*Has the Legislative Yuan, by enacting the Act of the Special Commission on the Investigation of the Truth in Respect of the 319 Shooting, Gone Beyond the Scope of Its Legislative Authorities? Are Any of the Relevant Provisions Contained Therein Unconstitutional?*" J.Y. Interpretation NO-585 12004J TWCC 15 (15 December 2004).

39 Council of Grand Justices, "Fingerprinting Decision": "*Are the Relevant Provisions of Article 8-II and III of the Household Registration Act, Stating to the Effect That the New ROC Identity Card Will Not Be Issued without the Applicant Being Fingerprinted, Unconstitutional?*" J.Y. Interpretation NO-603 [2005] TWCC 16 (28 September 2005).

40 *Mandatory Seatbelt Case,* Constitutional Court, 2003. 10. 30. 2002Hun-Ma518.
41 *Collecting and Computerizing Fingerprints and Using them for Investigation Purposes Case,* Constitutional Court, 2005. 5. 26. 2004Hun-Ma 190 (Consolidated).
42 *Real Namecase,* Constitutional Court, 2012.08.23 2010Hun-Ma47.
43 Joint News Release by LTA, IDA, and EZ-Link, *Near Field Communication-Enabled Mobile Phones Now Usable for Public Transport Payments,* available at: www.lta.gov.sg/apps/news/page.aspx?c=2&id=9a11347c-b41e-4831-8327-a422aa2a1878.
44 Speech Delivered by Mr Allan Chiang, Privacy Commissioner for Personal Data (Hong Kong) at Privacy Laws & Business, 24th Annual International Conference at St. John's College, Cambridge, UK (13 July 2011), available at: www.pcpd.org.hk/english/news_events/speech/files/speech_20110713.pdf.
45 *Ibid.*
46 See PCPD, *Report Published under Section 48(2) of the Personal data (Privacy) Ordinance* (Cap. 486), Report Number: R10-9866 (18 October 2010), available at: www.pcpd.org.hk/english/enforcement/commissioners_findings/investigation_reports/files/R10_9866_e.pdf. An *Interim Report on the Investigation Concerning Personal Data Collected and Disclosed under the Octopus Rewards Program* (30 July 2010) is also available at: www.pcpd.org.hk/english/publications/files/OctopusReport_e.pdf.
47 PCPD website (Investigative Reports), available at: www.pcpd.org.hk/english/enforcement/commissioners_findings/investigation_reports/invest_report.html.
48 EZ-Link, *EZ-Link and Taiwan's EasyCard Corporation Sign MoU to Develop Cross Border Combi Card* (2 June 2014), available at: http://home.ezlink.com.sg/2014/06/ez-link-and-taiwans-easycard-corporation-sign-mou-to-develop-cross-border-combi-card.
49 See Alabaster, Jay, *Backlash Occurs in Japan Over Sales of Train E-Ticket Records* (5 July 2013), available at: www.pcworld.com/article/2043706/backlash-in-japan-over-sales-of-train-eticket-records.html. See also Miyashita, Hiroshi, *Approve or Disapprove: Selling Suica Travel Records (The Japan News,* 2014), available at: www.yomiuri.co.jp/adv/chuo/dy/opinion/20140303.html.

6 Redefining the data economy

This chapter draws on the experimental work done on the transportation data in Singapore and the related legal analysis on privacy protection. The aim of the experiment was to highlight the challenges of obtaining data from public and private sources, performing analytics, and ensuring that the experiment as a whole lay within the acceptable perimeter of the prevailing legal boundaries. Going beyond the direct outcome of the analytics, there are also several features of data and its use that frame the structure of a new economy. These relate to how data is to be valued and how such valuation can be captured through a national accounts system. This is particularly salient in the current environment in which substantial amounts of data are being produced, stored, curated, and, in many instances, extracted for analysis that generates value. Equally, there are questions on the ownership of such data and the effect that its widespread use has on labour and economic relations. These concerns become all the more important when it is seen that the processes of data creation and use result in a redrawing of the contours of a growing marketplace. This expansion will have policy implications that affect a future labour market and the adoption of technology and require the recrafting of appropriate legislation and regulations.

Data search, analytics, and value creation

While data is being produced, collected, and used by a host of private and public entities, obtaining it for the purposes of analysis and insights is fraught with numerous constraints. In the experiment on transportation data in Singapore, it was observed that different legal obligations attended data held by private and public agencies. The data from private sources such as EZ-Link could only be obtained through an NDA. This is to be expected in most engagements with private entities where there is a commercial need to protect important strategic information. However, data from a public agency such as LTA is governed by the OSA, where the demands of confidentiality have no fixed time horizon. What is more telling is that each entity only collects what is required in the nature of their distinct operations; EZ-Link collects data pertinent to the needs of a financial transaction only, while LTA collects data that has a resonance with transport planning in terms of trips and trip lengths. The need to aggregate these different sets of data became apparent when it was noted that a combined data structure would give more valuable insights into specific market segments such as gender, age, and nature of traveller – tourist, senior citizen, etc. And, in order to maintain confidentiality, both sets of data were anonymised by their respective DPOs. This meant that a fair amount of detailed information embedded in the data became non-extractable. Nonetheless, an ingenious algorithm based on practical assumptions allowed for key insights to be drawn from the aggregated data sets. This implies that a good data science capability can overcome the veil of secrecy that shrouds different data sets, if used in a meaningful way.

The analytics provided several important insights. There has been, in Singapore, a vibrant debate on the merits and use of public transportation. A snapshot of the data sets has shown that both the bus and subway systems have an almost equal share of passenger volumes, with bus usage slightly ahead of the MRT. This may be as a result of the reconstituted bus routes and their seamless connectivity to the subway system at one level and the convenience of bus services at another. In both cases, the planning perspective must therefore become cognisant of the relative importance of the bus system and the prospects for its widening usage with or without connectivity to the subway system. Presumably, the new models of bus contracting services already take this into account and indicate the importance of bus services to the national transportation strategy.

The MRT data sets show that there are at least three important nodes within the network – Orchard, Bugis, and Jurong. Weekend traffic is highest at Orchard, while weekday traffic is highest at Jurong. Interestingly, these two stations are also located in areas with different profiles; Orchard is the entrance to the shopping and hotel belt, while Jurong is largely residential with a strong industrial and commercial annexure. When time-of-day analysis is done, such as on Bugis, it is seen that the heaviest traffic is between 12 p.m. and 5 p.m. on Saturdays. Similar analysis can be done for all of the stations within the network, allowing planners to design appropriate exigency strategies for the different stations by time of day. There is an inherent value in this process in that it allows for a rapid response for recovery in the event of a systemic failure, which, in turn, translates into cost containment.

The ability to segment this data into gender and age profiles is also important. In Bugis, for example, it is shown that the majority of MRT passengers alighting there are males aged between 20 and 39 years. This would indicate that the retail outlets there are likely to be of interest to men in this age group. It is also possible that Bugis acts as the catchment for the nearby electronics mall at Sim Lim Square as well. Placing these factors into context, it can be seen that there may be a preponderance of electronics and other male-interest attractions around this station. An analysis of Raffles Interchange may, however, show a different profile. These different profiles have commercial value to mall owners, credit card companies, and financial institutions. They can target their marketing campaigns by day of the week and time of day to attract the particular segments of foot traffic in these stations.

The heat maps of the movements of subway passengers show further insights into the dynamics of the transportation network. Senior citizens tend to be concentrated in the downtown area in the early hours of the morning, while students dominate the central and western parts of the island at that time. This is to be expected, since students leave their homes around these areas for school at that hour of the morning. The surprising feature is the presence of senior citizens in the downtown area at that hour. This may be a feature of the off-peak pricing system and the various other health-orientated activities that take place in the downtown green areas in the morning. For example, there are many senior citizens who participate in tai chi and physical exercise at Tanjong Pagar and Hong Lim Green in the early hours of the morning, and then commute to their homes after the peak period ends at 9 a.m. They thus have an incentive to use the system to get to these places before the peak period that starts at 6.30 a.m. Tourists, meanwhile, are most active in the evening hours of the weekends and mainly in the downtown area, implying that the restaurants and late shopping in that part of town are of importance on those days. Alternatively, it may also be a signal of the time at which they return to their hotels after a day out in other places such as Sentosa, the zoo, the Orchard shopping belt, and so on. Each of these heat maps, while providing some broad patterns of people's movements, raise interesting questions regarding what activities in the places around these stations are the catalysing factors for such movements of foot traffic. If these heat maps can be correlated to mobile phone data for the same time and place, this would provide further insights into which establishments in these areas are dominant at those times and, by inference, indicate the type of activity that animates the location.

The challenge, however, remains in how to value the information obtained from these insights. In Chapter 2, it was indicated that valuing personal data is a difficult task, and various models for this have been suggested. There is no agreed-upon way in which data can be valued, but the insights obtained from data analytics can be valued in some fashion. For example, the insights from the gender and time-of-day footfalls at Bugis could be marketed to different interested parties and a pricing profile obtained from the offers. There could also be an auction of the insights, applying different auction models. Other methods include statistical modelling, optimisation, and voting.[1] While these models, if adopted, would provide compensation to the seller, the more important issue is whether individuals will also get a share of the compensation, since it is their aggregated, and hopefully anonymised, data that is being sold. The Hong Kong experience shows that the travelling public may not take kindly to this data being sold for analytics, thereby making the sale of the insights even more tenuous. In the current circumstances, therefore, there seems to be a reluctance to monetise these insights. This state of affairs could change once the privacy laws on what can and cannot be done with aggregated and anonymised data are tested, as well as when the law decides on whether individuals can demand a share of their proportion of the revenue obtained from the sale of these insights.

A market for privacy and anonymity

Many of the concerns over big data and its use hinge on concerns over privacy and the confidentiality of personal information. The standard response to these issues is to have informed consent and, added to it, a layer of anonymisation. In the world of big data and analytics, data is acquired through monitoring, by collecting data as a by-product from other related activities, or by an active transfer from a specific set of information.[2] Informed consent in this context implies that the supplier of the data has agreed to the terms and conditions under which he or she is participating in a transaction. In the case of web-based services, for example, this means that the individual has read the webpages that state these requirements and that the individual then clicks on the "I agree" box, thereby allowing him or her to access the services being offered. This notion of consent and, there-fore, acceptance of some unilateral terms-of-service contracts can be seen as being one-sided. It also implies that somehow the individual has con-trol over his or her personal information. The truth, however, is that most people do not read the terms and conditions embedded in the inner pages of a website and, even if they do, they are not familiar with them. In effect, then, individuals are freely giving away their personal data on the premise that somehow it will be protected by the acquirer. This is also the case when individuals acquire a credit card, a phone card, or a transit card when they sign the terms of acquisition and usage.

This brings us to the idea of anonymisation. The two regularly used approaches for anonymisation are *k*-anonymity and differential privacy. Both are algorithmic approaches to ensuring that a particular individual cannot be identified from a data set. Even if these approaches are effective to a large extent, particular individuals may still be inferred from the different data sets if the sets can be overlaid.[3] Indeed, in the experiment on transportation data in this study, the aggregation of EZ-Link and LTA data and the use of algorithms based on specific assumptions allowed for market segmentation and identification of categories such as *tourists*. While the fit may not have been perfect, the fact that some clear patterns could be discerned implies that a more refined analytics could at some point identify specific individuals. More importantly, as technology improves and newer algorithms or methods of matching become available, the ability to identify individuals through a process of inference may become more prevalent and effective in the future. In the United States, for example, this process may be expedited further with the recent repeal of the law requiring ISPs to obtain the consent of customers before collecting and sharing their personal data.[4]

The relevance of privacy can be seen in the online purchase of products and services, for example, where the consumer's preferences become known to the merchant, who then aggregates and profiles the buying habits of a particular group of consumers. In such a transaction, the consumer has no control over how the data on his or her purchasing behaviour is put to use. It is a set of data points that attend the digital transaction but that, collectively, defines a specific profile. There may also be a market for transactions that depend on such personal data through intermediaries, such as the data locker companies outlined in Chapter 2. These companies may trade the data among themselves or with other entities. An extension of this form of transaction is the provision of personal data by a consumer in return for free products or services provided by a web-based company, search engines, or social networks. In this instance, the price for providing the data is almost negligible. The use of transportation data from those who have registered their cards in the ez-link system in Singapore can be considered as being from this class of consumer. Once their details have been captured by the system, all of their subsequent movements on the subway and bus systems, and some purchases, are easily captured in the transaction data that EZ-Link processes. If permitted, this data can be traded with other firms. This is termed a "market for personal data."[5] There may also be a market for privacy,[6] in which individuals seek specific ways of protecting their personal information through products and services available in the marketplace. This could be, for example, a browser protector that erases all traces of web browsing sites when the system is used. As individuals begin to perceive the value of their own profiles, they may then have a desire to extract a price from those wishing to access them. Data locker companies have, in response, developed various business models for these services to individuals.[7]

Within the world of privacy and anonymisation, there is thus the emergence of different product types, players, and forms of exchange. In short, there is now a market mechanism that is being formed for trading in privacy. Much of the behaviour in this marketplace is being governed by the rules of privacy that draw inspiration from the idea of "informed consent." However, as detailed in Chapter 5, this may not be sufficient. The public at large may desire to have some control over how their personal data is being used. If this is so, then the idea of informed consent may be contestable at some point in the future, especially if advances in technology can generate different methods of inference to identify individuals from seemingly anonymised data. In a data-driven world, therefore, it will be necessary to have institutions, incentives, laws, technologies, or norms about which information flows are permitted or prevented and which are encouraged or discouraged.[8]

A question of measurement

It is a now a reality that digital technology and the use of data have become features of the modern economy. However, they contribute to national welfare in unusual ways. For example, while it may have been possible to value the purchase of a book or a magazine and have the measurement of this minor activity reflected in GDP, the same product when shared or streamed at almost negligible cost across the Internet cannot be so easily quantified. The industry that most closely shows how this has now transformed the economy is entertainment. The streaming of music and films has changed the way in which these services are delivered to consumers. There is inherently more sharing of the products or services that are streamed or downloaded. Similarly, new technology such as WhatsApp allows communication at very low or no cost. Increasingly, products and services are being delivered through mobile phones, tablets, and laptops at a negligible price. Without doubt, these deliverables add value to the economy by satisfying consumer wants, yet this true value is not captured in the national accounts. The traditional metrics used in computing domestic GDP are unable to capture these features.[9] There is, as a result, a loosening of the relationship between national welfare and the measurements that have traditionally defined it. This effect is expected to increase as the "sharing economy" becomes commonplace.

The enabler of the "sharing economy" is technology and data analytics. In this economy, each individual offers to share his or her products with others for some compensation. The manner in which the offer and acceptance works is through social networks or an Internet marketplace. The digital platforms on which these transactions take place are repositories of vast amounts of data pertaining to those products and services, those offering them, and those partaking of them. The platform thus acts as a "clearing house" and, in that process, accumulates a significant amount of data on the transactions and participants. An owner of the social network platform can thus profile the participants and their interests in different products and services and, if necessary, tailor the platform for different forms of transactions – free exchange, segmented fees, and so on. Much of this data cannot be accounted for through the measurement of GDP at present.

There are other features of a data economy that have now caused an erosion of GDP as a measure of national wealth. Digital processes that underpin the data economy allow more people to be self-employed or become freelance workers. They have flexible work habits, with multitasking becoming an almost everyday feature. Many are using household assets such as computers, mobile phones, and their cars for paid work.[10] This is also known as non-marketed output, the value of which is not imputed in the computation of GDP.[11] These trends will amplify as technology evolves at a faster pace.

In the case of the experiment on transportation in Singapore, it has been shown that rich insights can be extracted from aggregated data sets. Unless a market for these insights is created, they are less likely to be reflected in the computation of national income. A form of exchange of this information that establishes its price is needed for it to be identified as a digital transaction for value. This means that the data and the analytics that follow it have to be valued in some manner. In essence, datafication requires a method of valuation so that eventually the processes that use the data can be seen as a part of a production line with distinct outputs of a certain value. When this capability is created, standardised, and accepted, the value of data and its transactions will be more easily reconciled within measurements of national income.

The new labour market

In the data economy, there will be a greater demand for better-skilled workers. The definition of "skill" in this context also has to be appreciated to have a sense of the wider implications of this change. Here, "skill" implies not just dexterity and artful manual capability, but a more deeply trained mind that allows for interaction with machines, software, and related applications. This requires a new approach to skills formation with a facility in science and technology.

On the factory floor, skilled workers will be those who are able to read and interpret data outputs and analytics that provide a detailed view of the operations of robots and other automated machinery. They will have to reprogram machines, monitor their performance, and liaise with programmers and engineers in the control centre to ensure improved efficiency. When there is a larger degree of industrial automation with machine learning at the forefront, the skills needed will increase even more. Then they will have to understand how the machine learning process is affecting the production line and how and when they should intervene when tolerances go beyond the acceptable range. These are specialised skills requiring technical skills, not manual dexterity. The age of the manual assembly line is at an end.

In the service sector, for example, the advent of voice recognition technology and the emergence of more efficient algorithms will shift the roles of many workers. New high-speed computing at cheap costs and better speeds through network communications using compression technology will make this change more rapid and reliable. Banking facilities, bill payments, airline bookings, and call centre activities, for example, all stand to become machine-driven once voice recognition technology becomes an established feature of the service industry. This change in how technology and data are being used will also affect the "professional" establishment of lawyers, accountants, and doctors.

In medicine, the availability of large data sets of anonymised patients already allows medical researchers to identify patterns of illnesses and their successful treatment modalities and set new benchmarks for illness tracking.[12] This ability can then be combined with individual treatment plans drawn from genomics data to ensure that the efficacy of the treatment is greatly improved. Similarly, the technology to sift through vast amounts of case law, judgements, and awards makes it easier for law firms to take a position on their clients' cases. This will eventually reduce the number of lawyers and paralegals engaged in background research. How and when this will affect advocacy in the courts remains to be seen, however. Nevertheless, legal opinion can now be based on insights derived from large data sets on case law.[13] The accountancy profession probably faces the greatest challenge as digitisation and datafication make their jobs obsolete. As more companies automate their accounts, integrate their operational and accounting data, and adhere to standard accounting practices, the need for accountants within firms will be reduced. More importantly, the need for outsourced accounting services will also reduce in importance. This will become more visible as tax authorities move into predictive taxation practices in which large data sets and historical trends allow them to forecast individual company and personal taxes with greater accuracy.[14]

What is clear from these examples is that automation together with big data is not just displacing workers in repetitive tasks; it is also having an impact on middle managers and professions. The new workforce is more skill- and knowledge-intensive, while the workforce itself is shrinking and adapting to the technology-driven workplace. At one level, there will be a growing demand for data scientists and those with specialised skills in programming, cybersecurity, and data management, while at another, there will be a decrease in demand for those in the traditional skills such as sales, marketing, product management, and the like. This displacement will have a bias in that the new data science workers will be of a smaller number than that of the displaced traditional workers. In short, data science employment is unlikely to create sizeable growth in the labour market, but instead have an overall depressing effect as automation and big data become prevalent. There will be a decrease in the overall demand for labour as these technological capabilities are adopted by the different economic sectors. Automation will in itself reduce the labour component in industry and services, with a call for higher skills. Yet, this very change will then be subject to the use of big data, analytics, machine learning, and other sophisticated methods that will enhance the capabilities of automation and restrict labour growth even further. In effect, the rapid growth in technology and its uses will result in labour displacement, with only a smaller proportion of it being replaced. This structural change is known as "technological unemployment," which is due to the discovery of means of economising the use of labour outrunning the pace at which we can find new uses for labour.[15]

In a city such as Singapore, this effect could have dramatic consequences, as the impact of technology will be felt most acutely in the service sector, which contributed just over 69% of GDP in 2016.[16] While it is accepted that automation in manufacturing is taking place with regularity, it is less obvious in the service sector at present. Employment in services is currently around 84% of the total labour force, and about a third of this service sector employment is in business, finance, insurance, and infocomm services.[17] These are also the economic areas most amenable to a wider use of automation, big data, and analytics. Thus, the dislocation in this segment of the labour market as a result of technology adoption may be more severe, and happen sooner, than envisaged.

There is a paradox in how these technology-induced changes affect the economy. The various data-driven applications, for example, provide consumers with a wide variety of services and products at low cost. Meanwhile, globalisation and better connectivity will strengthen the economies of scale within a short time frame because of network effects, leading to significant wealth creation. Yet, these rewards accrue to only a small group of people who are inventive enough to develop these services. Thus, one of the effects of a data economy is the wider divergence in income that will arise between those who have the capital and skills and those who are mere wage earners. Mismatches in the labour market will therefore exacerbate income disparities even more.

The changing structure

The research in this study began with an outline of what a data economy would look like. What is clear from the analytical work that has been done is that the participants in the segments that constitute the marketplace are undergoing change. Within the private sector, for example, there has been the emergence of data aggregators, data analytics providers, and other service segments that animate the "sharing economy." At a broader level, however, more data is being produced and used. While governments continue to be important producers and participants in this process, the private sector and individuals will probably become the larger suppliers and users of data. As data becomes a readily usable commodity for productive decision-making and adds significant value to market participants, it begins to have a transforming capability resembling historical innovations such as steam power and electricity; it becomes a "general purpose technology."[18] This is defined as "deep new ideas or techniques that have the potential for important impacts on many sectors of the economy."[19]

Indeed, data is becoming a ubiquitous feature of most activities as its capture, storage, and analysis is becoming cheaper and more efficient each day. As described in Chapter 2, the variety and complexity of data are also growing rapidly. There are visual images, texts, digital forms, and, now with voice recognition technology, audio clips that make up different types of data. Equally important is that these data sets are being captured through numerous technologies such as video cameras, sensors, microphones, magnetic strips, RFID chips, and others. These are also being transmitted to central servers on a continuous and real-time basis at high speeds using data compression techniques and better hardware. This proliferation of data in different forms, when stored, curated, and standardised, allows for systematic analysis using sophisticated algorithms. More importantly, even the design of algorithms is being done by machines learning through feedback, automatic corrections, and refinements.

In this expanded market for the production and use of data, there arises the question of privacy of individuals and firms and the attendant issue of cybersecurity. There are already various technical methods of ensuring data privacy, as outlined earlier. This is being augmented by legal requirements for consent regarding the use of data and restrictions, or otherwise, on firms on how they can use the collected data from individuals. In some jurisdictions, there is less oversight and a greater degree of self-regulation by firms operating in this sector of the economy. Nevertheless, the growth and use of data as a general purpose technology bring with them specific responsibilities on maintaining privacy. The role of government in legislating and enforcing rules and regulations is therefore likely to expand, just as there will be a deepening of the technology for analytics and privacy management. In addition, the impact on skills and labour due to improvements in technology will also require a public sector response to ensure employment creation and more equitable income distribution. Taken as a whole, then, the role of government is likely to expand and deepen in the data

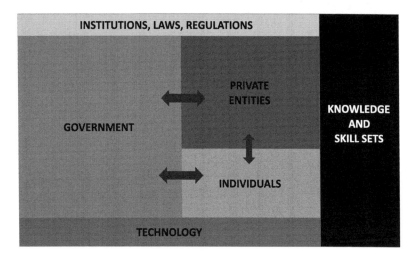

Figure 6.1 Transformation of the marketplace
Note: The arrows indicate data flows
Source: Authors

economy, even as its shares of the production and use of this general purpose technology are reduced.

Figure 6.1 reflects the changes that define the marketplace when
compared to those shown earlier in Figure 2.2 in Chapter 2. The bolder
borders indicate the strengthening of these features as the data economy
becomes a visible reality.

Several features stand out in the transformation of the economy. Private
entities and individuals become bigger players in the marketplace, providing
a wider spectrum of data and data-based transactions. Governments' share in
this marketplace may become smaller, even as the overall market increases
significantly. The growth in non-public sector data will be a function of the
deepening and hardening of technology and its related skill sets. As newer
technologies come on stream and better algorithms are instituted, the ability
of the private sector and individuals to create and sustain new services and
products will increase rapidly. The public sector, in order to keep abreast
of these developments, will also call upon a wider skill set and more technology to participate in and police the new contours of the economy. But
this alone will not be enough. The public sector will be called upon to set
up institutions, improve regulatory oversight, and institute new laws to prevent abuses of the marketplace and transactions. The need for a fair and

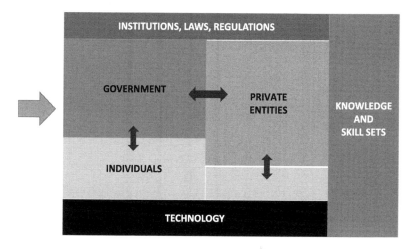

Figure 6.1 Cont.

transparent market that is being veiled through technology, algorithms, and other techniques will demand a greater say from the government in how the public interest should be protected. Indeed, this has already become obvious in the wake of the Facebook data breach[20] and the ensuing demands for greater privacy protection. So, in summary, it may be observed that the new marketplace will experience significant government intervention through institutions, laws, and regulations buttressed by the use of technology and enhanced skills.

Notes

1 Iyer, Bala, "Valuing the Data Asset," Babson College, Boston, slideshare.net, 20 June 2014.
2 Strandburg, Katherine J., "Monitoring, Datafication and Consent: Legal Approaches to Privacy in the Big Data Context,", in J. Lane et al., *Privacy, Big Data, and the Public Good*, Cambridge University Press, New York, 2014.
3 Barocas, Solon and Helen Nissenbaum, "Big Data's End Run around Anonymity and Consent," *Ibid.*
4 S.J. Res 34, 3 April 2017.
5 Acquisti, Alessandro, "The Economics and Behavioral Economics of Privacy," in J. Lane et al., 2014.
6 *Ibid.*
7 Ctrl-Shift, 2014.
8 Brynjolfsson, Erik and Andrew McAfee, *The Second Machine Age*, W.W. Norton, New York, 2014, p. 253.

 9 Varian, Hal, "Intelligent Technology," *Finance & Development*, World Bank, Washington, DC, September 2016
10 Coyle, Diane, "Rethinking GDP," *Finance & Development,* World Bank, Washington, DC, March 2017.
11 Chang, Ha-Joon, *Economics: The User's Guide*, Pelican, London, 2014, pp. 215–216.
12 Marr, Bernard, "How Big Data is Changing Healthcare," 21 April 2015, forbes.com.
13 Marr, Bernard, "How Big Data Is Disrupting Law Firms and the Legal Profession," 20 January 2016, forbes.com.
14 Peccarelli, Brian, "How the Cloud Is Unlocking the Predictive Power of Tax Data," 8 August 2016, www2.cfo.com.
15 Keynes, J.M., *Essays in Persuasion,* W.W. Norton, New York, 1963. p. 358, as given in Brynjolfsson, 2014.
16 Singapore Statistics, 2017.
17 Total employment in Singapore was 2.165 million in 2016. *Ibid.*
18 Brynjolfsson, 2014. P. 76.
19 Wright, Gavin, "Review of Helpman (1998)," *Journal of Economic Literature* 2000, 20:161–162, as given in Brynjolfsson, 2014.
20 *The Guardian*, 8 April 2018.

7 Implications for the future

A new market structure is now emerging, with data becoming an important feature of this development. Technology and new skills are also important drivers of this new contour. Paradoxically, these movements also call upon greater vigilance and intervention by governments to ensure transparency and fairness. Individuals and businesses stand to gain much from how this new "data economy" becomes a part of daily life. More so, a new generation of young, technology-literate individuals is poised to capitalise on this changing marketplace. It also calls for a different way of assessing and managing production and services for the future, while adhering to new demands for privacy and confidentiality in how transactions are executed.

The strategic imperative

A data ecosystem now exists with firms, individuals, and governments participating at various levels. The new economy has begun to use data as a value-generating commodity in addition to traditional products and services. In this environment, it is important to understand the connectivity among the different participants, their economic interests, and the possible bottlenecks that could prevent a more efficient system from being created. There are three critical strategic considerations that need to be addressed in the immediate term:

> *Understand network effects and how the ensuing connectivity among the participants creates value* by having metrics that can capture data flows and their value to the information production process. This calls for a better appreciation of how firms and individuals trade data between and among themselves and how network effects compound this value-generating activity. It requires a disaggregation of the structure of the market participants to see more clearly how the value chain is being constructed and

the manner in which data flows animate them. Measurement of data, its analytics, and its value will thus have to become standard features in economic activities. This calls for a new mindset in perceiving business operations and personal transactions. It requires an understanding of data, its usefulness, business processes, and how individuals generate and use data. Meanwhile, the IoT and new forms of connectivity such as through mobile phones, digital wristwatches, autonomous vehicles, and the like are producing significant amounts of data on a continuous basis. This is being further augmented by data uploads into social networks in the form of photographs, texts, and audio and visual clips. How these different data streams feed into the various market participants, how they analyse and use the data streams, and what value they derive from them are important questions that need to be addressed in this endeavour.

Analyse the new economic structure and its emerging contours through the use of these better metrics that capture data flows and the presence of different participants. The structure of the marketplace is in a constant state of flux, as existing large players cause market concentration and new entrants operate in niche areas. The combination of these effects is to have rapid change in market structure as mergers, acquisitions, and natural business attrition occur. It will be essential to understand how this market structure is changing and how different business models are being used to generate wealth. This will allow a deeper appreciation of the effects of technology and data analytics on labour and income. It will permit the assessment of policy choices on how income disparities should be reduced as better skills and capital displace more of the labour in both manufacturing and services. Central to this question will also be the creation of different workforms to absorb displaced labour from the market. The nature of work will change in tandem with changes in market structure, and new skills will be needed to fill available jobs. Many of these will require adaptable and creative abilities. This then leads to questions on the appropriate education and training that have to be imparted to a younger generation of students and future workers. Going further, these changes raise important policy choices on how society and social interactions should function in an electronically connected world.

Evaluate, identify, and resolve potential bottlenecks in the new economy through an active process of monitoring economic activities driven by data and its analytics. A legislative environment that balances fair and free trade with protection of privacy has to be in place to allow seamless transactions. This also calls for the strong hand of government and the courts to police the four corners of the marketplace by enforcing rules and regulations without bias. As a part of this responsibility, both the public and private agents in the marketplace will have to be accountable for the protection of data and the prevention of breaches through weaknesses in cybersecurity. The technical capabilities required for preventing cyberattacks and breaches in data privacy have to be buttressed with laws, rules, and regulations that provide for sanctions against abuse or misuse. Just as important as preventing bottlenecks will be the need to ensure sufficient capacity for data usage. This means that forward planning for improving hardware and infrastructure in order to achieve better and more reliable connectivity will be a constant requirement. This is no different from ensuring that other general purpose technologies, such as electricity, will always be available, since data will also have to be accepted as a similar technology with multiple uses. A philosophy of building ahead of demand may be necessary to ensure that sufficient "bandwidth" is always available and to allow for data to become a part of the bed-rock that defines economic activities.

Facing the future

The data economy poses several challenges for policy-makers. In the short term, the rapid changes in technology and its adoption will cause labour dislocation. Finding replacement jobs to absorb this surplus labour will be a demanding concern. It will not be easy to retrain older workers to take on work requiring quantitative and creative skills. More significantly, layers of managerial and professional work will become obsolete in the data economy. These workers will have to become self-employed or become self-reliant in other ways. In Singapore, anecdotal evidence shows that many have taken up taxi-driving or have become Uber and Grab drivers. Some younger displaced workers have opted to be retrained in the hope of finding alternative employment. Other alternatives may need to be explored, including more supportive financing schemes for different small-scale entrepreneurial activities.

The effects of the "sharing economy" have to be better understood. Airbnb lets, equipment sharing, and other models of social behaviour are changing the ways in which economic transactions are being crafted. In Singapore, the subletting of owner-occupied public housing for those who have been displaced in the labour market may have to be thought through carefully. The sharing model may not be appropriate when social housing forms a significant portion of the housing stock. In other areas, the sharing economy can play an important role. For example, the sharing of transportation through taxi apps for sharing rides or group travel in the autonomous vehicles of the future have significant advantages in terms of cost containment and environmental improvement.

In the longer term, there will be a confluence of several factors that will affect the economic structure of a city such as Singapore. An ageing population will make increasing demands on the public purse through a need for better social protection and enhanced skills and training for those who are able to work. There will be constant churn in the employment market as technology disrupts and makes obsolete once-important functions. The services sector will see new jobs being created while many others are removed. At the same time, new services in small-scale enterprises may grow. Some of these jobs will be at high wages, while at the lower levels, increasing competition will drive down wages. In short, owners of capital and skills will have higher returns than those who are workers. Income disparity may, therefore, become more apparent. Technology adoption, new data science approaches, and improved communications will, in the meantime, make economic transactions more secure and reliable. This will change the way in which people will consume their incomes. The role of governments in ensuring a fair playing field will become all the more important in this environment where there is the possibility of "winner takes all."

Selected bibliography

Ayres, Ian, *Super Crunchers*, John Murray, London, 2008.

Brian Arthur, W, *The Nature of Technology*, Free Press, New York, 2009.

Brynjolfsson, Erik and Andrew McAfee, *The Second Machine Age*, W.W. Norton, New York, 2014.

Chang, Ha-Joon, *Economics: The User's Guide*, Pelican, London, 2014.

Davenport, Thomas, *Big Data @ Work*, HBR Press, Boston, MA, 2014.

Franks, Bill, *The Analytics Revolution*, Wiley, New Jersey, 2014.

Ford, Martin, *The Lights in the Tunnel*, Acculant, New York, 2009.

Ford, Martin, *The Rise of the Robots*, Basic Books, New York, 2015.

Lohr, Steve, *Data-ism: Inside the Big Data Revolution*, Oneworld, London, 2015.

Mayer-Schonberger, Viktor and Kenneth Cuiker, *Big Data*, John Murray, London, 2013.

McEwen, Adrian and Hakim Casimally, *Designing the Internet of Things*, Wiley, West Sussex, 2014.

Parker, Geoffrey, Marshall W. Van Alstyne, and Sangeet Paul Choudary, *Platform Revolution*, W.W. Norton, New York, 2016.

Provost, Foster and Tom Fawcett, *Data Science for Business*, O'Reilly, Sebastopol, CA, 2013.

Sundararajan, Arun, *The Sharing Economy*, MIT Press, Cambridge, MA, 2016.

Tapscott, Don, *The Digital Economy*, McGraw-Hill, New York, 2015.

Index

For Product Safety Concerns and Information please contact our EU
representative GPSR@taylorandfrancis.com Taylor & Francis Verlag GmbH,
Kaufingerstraße 24, 80331 München, Germany

Printed and bound by CPI Group (UK) Ltd, Croydon, CR0 4YY

11/04/2025

01844008-0007